Strange
and Fascinating Facts
About
the Royal Family

Strange and Fascinating Facts About the Royal Family

Graham and Heather Fisher

BELL PUBLISHING COMPANY
New York

Published 1985 by Bell Publishing Company,
distributed by Crown Publishers, Inc. by
arrangement with Graham and Heather Fisher.

Printed and bound in the United States of America

**Library of Congress Cataloging in Publication
Data**

Fisher, Graham.
  Strange and fascinating facts about the royal
family.

    1. Elizabeth II, Queen of Great Britain, 1926–
—Family. 2. Windsor, House of I. Fisher,
Heather. II. Title.
DA590.F533   1985   941.085   85-6170

ISBN: 0-517-474670

h g f e d c b a

Contents

A Royal Who's Who 1
What's in a Name? 5
Bloodlines 17
Purely Personal 29
A la Carte 53
Love and Marriage 67
Jokers Royal 91
Upstairs, Downstairs 105
Royal Duty 117
Palace Secrets 139
The Royal Road Show 157
Money Matters 179
Fashion Notes 197
Royal Memoirs 211
War Diary 221
Close Encounters of the Royal Kind . . 231
Wit and Wisdom 243
Royal Firsts 255
Historical Footnotes 261

A Royal Who's Who

Elizabeth II—Queen of England, Scotland, Wales, and Northern Ireland along with seventeen other countries around the world, from vast landmasses like Canada and Australia to islands in the Pacific that are mere pinpoints on the map. Born 1926, married 1947, became queen 1952, crowned 1953. A conscientious, sometimes obstinate woman who puts her royal duty before everything else.

Prince Philip—Elizabeth's tall, handsome, wittily outspoken, and sometimes tetchy husband. Born 1921.

Charles, Prince of Wales—Elizabeth's eldest son and Britain's future king. Ex-naval officer, pilot, enthusiastic polo player, and fox hunter, among other things. Born 1948, married 1981.

Diana, Princess of Wales—Charles' tall and delectable wife and Britain's future queen. Born 1961.

Prince William of Wales—Charles and Diana's firstborn son and therefore Britain's next-but-one king (after Charles). Born 1982.

Prince Henry of Wales—Charles and Diana's second born son and heir to the throne after Prince William. Born 1984.

Princess Anne—Elizabeth's second child and only daughter. Born 1950, married 1973. Mad on horses. A no-nonsense lady who works incredibly hard for her favorite charity, the Save the Children Fund.

Captain Mark Phillips—Anne's husband. Ex-cavalry officer. As mad on horses as she is. Born 1948.

Peter and Zara Phillips—Children of Anne and Mark. Peter was born 1977 and Zara 1981.

Prince Andrew—Elizabeth's third child and second son. A lofty, handsome six-footer with an eye for the girls. Known to his friends as "Randy Andy." Born 1960 and currently a naval helicopter pilot who narrowly escaped being shot down by an Exocet missile during the Falklands campaign.

Prince Edward—Youngest of Elizabeth's brood and another six-footer but much shier than brother Andrew. Born 1964.

The Queen Mother—Elizabeth's mother, also named Elizabeth. Born 1900 and still a real charmer in her eighties.

King George VI—Elizabeth's father. Died of cancer and a coronary thrombosis in 1952.

Princess Margaret—Elizabeth's sister. Has had a turbulent and often unhappy love life. Born 1930, married 1960, divorced 1978.

Earl of Snowdon (usually called Tony Snowdon)—Margaret's professional photographer ex-husband. Married again six months after his divorce from Margaret. Actual name: Antony Armstrong-Jones.

David, Viscount Linley and Lady Sarah Armstrong-Jones—Margaret and Tony's children. David was born 1961 and Sarah 1964

2

Earl and Countess Spencer–Diana's father and step-mother. She is the daughter of romance novelist Barbara Cartland.

Hon. Frances Shand-Kydd—Diana's mother. She and Earl Spencer divorced when Diana was a child.

Charles, Viscount Althorp (pronounced *Al-thrup*)—Diana's brother.

Lady Sarah McCorquodale } Diana's sisters
Lady Jane Fellowes

Richard, Duke of Gloucester
Edward, Duke of Kent
Princess Alexandra of Kent } Elizabeth's cousins
Prince Michael of Kent
Earl of Harewood
Hon. Gerald Lascelles

Princess Alice of Gloucester—Elizabeth's aunt. Born 1901.

Duke of Windsor—Elizabeth's uncle. Reigned for less than a year in 1936 as King Edward VIII before abdicating to marry Wallis Simpson, a twice-divorced American. Died 1972.

Duchess of Windsor—Windsor's widow and Elizabeth's aunt by marriage. Previously married to Ernest Simpson and Earl Winfield Spencer (no relation to Diana's father despite the similarity of name), a U.S. naval lieutenant. Born at Blue Ridge Summit, PA, 1896.

Earl Mountbatten of Burma—Philip's uncle. Allied supreme commander in South East Asia during World War II. Murdered by the IRA while on vacation in Ireland in 1979.

King George V—Elizabeth's grandfather. Died 1936.

3

Queen Mary—Elizabeth's grandmother. Died 1953.

King Edward VII—Elizabeth's womanizing great-grandfather. Died 1910.

Queen Alexandra—Elizabeth's great-grandmother and long-suffering wife of Edward VII. Died 1925.

Queen Victoria—Great-great-grandmother of both Elizabeth and Philip. A formidable matriarch. Died 1901 at the age of eighty-one.

Prince Albert—Victoria's intellectual husband. Was only forty-two when he died of typhoid in 1861, leaving Victoria so heartbroken that people called her "The Widow of Windsor."

What's in a Name?

Queen Elizabeth II's full name is Elizabeth Alexandra Mary Windsor. To avoid confusion with her mother, who is also Queen Elizabeth, she is called "Lilibet" by others of the family, a diminutive deriving from her first lisping attempts to say her own name. Philip, by way of a change, sometimes calls her "Sweetie." She is "Mummy" to her children, "Ma'am" to even her friends and "Your Majesty" to everyone else.

*

Thanks to a draftsman who got his quill pens in a twist when drawing up her official title, she is not simply Queen Elizabeth II or even Queen of the United Kingdom. Instead, her offical designation is convoluted in the extreme: "Elizabeth the Second by the Grace of God of the United Kingdom of Great Britain and Northern Ireland and Her Other Realms and Territories Queen." She signs official documents *Elizabeth R* (for Regina).

*

The natives of Papua New Guinea, one of the seventeen other countries of which Elizabeth is also queen, speak a quaint dialect called pidgin English. Among them she has the much simpler title of "Misis Kwin." Prince Philip, in pidgin, is 'Nambawan (number one) Fella Blong Misis

Kwin," while Prince Charles is "Nambawan Pikini
(number-one pickaninny) Blong Misis Kwin."

*

Prince Philip was born Philippos Schleswig-Holstein-
Sonderberg-Glucksburg, Prince of Greece. Philippos
became Philip during schooldays in England. The other
boys nicknamed him "Flop" (Ph'lip-Flop, get it?). Exiled
from Greece, he was still technically a prince and was
brought up to sign his name simply as *Philip* in the royal
tradition. This led to trouble at times. There was nearly a
punch-up while renting a car in wartime Australia when the
dealer thought Philip was trying to con him. A nightclub
receptionist in London was less belligerent but similarly
suspicious when he signed in merely as "Philip."

"I'm afraid we require your surname, sir," she said.

Philip obliged by adding "of Greece."

"A joke is a joke, sir," said the receptionist, "but that
isn't a surname."

Fortunately, the couple with Philip at the time intervened
to explain.

*

Philip of Greece became plain Philip Mountbatten when
he relinquished his Greek title to take British citizenship
prior to marrying Elizabeth. His own choice of name was
actually Philip Oldcastle, but he was finally prevailed upon
to take the Mountbatten surname of his mother's family.
Elizabeth's father wanted to make him a Prince of the
United Kingdom, but Philip declined with thanks.
However, King George VI was not going to have his
daughter marry a mere naval lieutenant, and a few days
before the wedding he gave Philip the title Duke of
Edinburgh. But by then the order of service for the wedding
was already being printed, and Philip was still listed in it on
his wedding day as Lieutenant Philip Mountbatten. From

then on, everyone again referred to him as "Prince Philip," though in fact he did not become a prince again until his wife made him one in 1957. She usually calls him "Darling" in private, and he is "Papa" to his sons and daughter. His aides address him as "Sir." To everyone else, he is—or should be—"Your Royal Highness" the first time he is addressed and "Sir" thereafter.

*

Philip's occupation is given on his passport as "Prince of the Royal Household," but he is down on the Civil List, which stipulates how much money each royal receives, simply as "Husband of the Queen." His full official title is: His Royal Highness the Prince Philip, Duke of Edinburgh, Earl of Merioneth, and Baron Greenwich. He has a shoal of lesser titles, ranks, and designations. In America he is an Admiral of the Great Navy of the State of Nebraska, Grand Commander of the San Francisco Port Authority, Honorary Deputy Sheriff of Los Angeles County, Colonel of the Honorable Order of Kentucky Colonels, a member of the Confederate Air Force of Harlingen, Texas, and an honorary member of the Honorable Artillery Company of Massachusetts.

*

To Elizabeth's children, the queen mother is "Granny" and Princess Margaret is "Margo." Margaret would have been Ann if her parents had had their way when she was born. They wanted to name her Ann Margaret, but her grandfather, bluff old King George V, did not like the name. So Ann Margaret became Margaret Rose. "She isn't really a rose," lisped the four-year-old Elizabeth when she first saw her baby sister. "Just a bud."

*

King George V was long dead when Elizabeth herself had a daughter in 1950. So Charles' baby sister could be named Anne Elizabeth Alice Louise without any further fussing. Prince Charles' full names are Charles Philip Arthur George, a mouthful that Diana got the wrong way around on their wedding day. It was Philip Charles Arthur George instead of Charles Philip Arthur George she ended up taking as her lawful wedded husband. "You married my father," Charles teased her after the ceremony.

*

Charles' full title, like his name, is a mouthful—Prince of Wales and Earl of Chester, Duke of Cornwall and Duke of Rothesay, Earl of Carrick and Baron Renfrew, Lord of the Isles, and Great Steward of Scotland. To the Blackfoot and Blood tribes of Canada he is "Chief Red Crow." He signs himself *Charles P.* (for Prince). William calls him "Daddy," which Diana prefers to the more traditional royal "Papa." In a teasing moment she herself once called Charles "Fishface." Usually she calls him "Darling" and he calls her "Diana Love," though the cake he had made in Edmonton, Alberta, to celebrate her twenty-second birthday was iced with the romantic words, *I love you, Darling.*

Their sons' names are William Arthur Philip Louis and Henry Charles Albert David. Their official titles are Prince William of Wales and Prince Henry of Wales, but to their parents they are simply "Wills" and "Harry."

*

Charles is much less concerned about titles than he used to be. "This is Charles," his nanny once said to an artist who had been commissioned to paint his portrait. "This is *Prince* Charles," a small piping voice corrected her. He was not quite three at the time. But there was no fuss over the question of title during his years in the navy. He was happy enough for his fellow officers to address him simply as "Wales." Correctly speaking, like his father, he should be addressed as "Your Royal Highness" the first time and

"Sir" thereafter, but these days he is happy enough if people he chats to during royal walkabouts refer to him simply as "Charles" or even "Charlie." He and Diana were "Chuck and Di" to many Canadians during their 1983 tour of that country, while in Australia their small son was hailed as "Billy the Kid." But Charles does not particularly care for the American custom of addressing him as "Prince." "It makes me sound like a police dog," he says.

*

If Charles is less interested in titles than he was in childhood, Anne is more so. As a schoolgirl she was content to label her schoolbooks simply *P. Anne*. There was an occasion in her schooldays when she went on a brass-rubbing expedition to a nearby church, and an elderly gent fell into conversation with her. He asked her name.

"Windsor," she told him.

"Where are you from?" he asked.

"Windsor," said Anne again.

"Fancy that," chuckled the old man. "So you're Miss Windsor from Windsor."

These days Anne leaves people in no doubt as to who she is. When a photographer in Australia called out, "Look this way, love," she snapped back, "I am not your 'love.' I am Your Royal Highness."

*

Anne's full married name is Anne Elizabeth Alice Louise Phillips. Her children are Peter Mark Andrew Phillips and Zara Anne Elizabeth Phillips. Anne considerably outstrips her husband when it comes to titles. While she retains her title of princess, he has only his old army rank of captain. Unlike Princess Margaret's ex-husband, the Earl of Snowdon, Mark was not given a title when he married a royal. He did not want one, he said.

*

9

Because Mark has no title, the couple's children do not have titles either. Unlike their small cousins, William and Henry who were both born Princes of Wales, Anne and Mark's offspring are plain Peter and Zara Phillips, though their royal grandmother may make them a lord and lady later so that they do not feel inferior.

With the exception of Elizabeth's, royal titles are handed down only through the males of the family—however unfair that may seem in these days of sexual equality. Princess Margaret's children get their titles of Viscount Linley and Lady Sarah not from their mother but from their father, thanks to the fact that Elizabeth made him an earl when he married her sister.

Just as Anne's children have no titles because their father does not have one, neither do the children of Elizabeth's cousin, Alexandra, though their cousins, the children of Alexandra's two brothers, do. While Alexandra herself is a princess, her husband—and the father of the children—is an untitled businessman, Angus Ogilvy.

*

Strictly speaking, even Diana has no royal title of her own. She was Lady Diana in bachelor-girl days because her father is an earl. But she was not born royal, as her in-laws, Margaret and Anne, were. So she is not really "Princess Diana" in the sense that Princess Margaret and Princess Anne are. Because she is royal only by marriage, she is dependent on her husband for her title and should correctly be called "Princess of Wales."

The wives of Elizabeth's male Gloucester and Kent cousins are similarly royal only by marriage and so take their husbands' titles to become Duchess of Gloucester, Duchess of Kent, and the curiously styled Princess Michael of Kent.

Princess Michael's real name is Marie-Christine, though

others of the family know her as "Our Val" because of her Valkyrie-like attitude. Palace servants spring stiffly to attention when she comes to call and "dinner with Princess Michael," Margaret's son jokes, is what he would wish on his worst enemy.

*

Like many another career woman, Elizabeth II clings to her maiden name, which is Windsor. She became a Mountbatten when she married Philip in 1947, but reverted to her own name soon after becoming Queen in 1952. Her prime minister at the time was that tough old war horse, Winston Churchill. A man with no great love for the Mountbatten family into which she had married, he prevailed upon her to revert to her maiden name. Her change of name, made legal by a royal decree, also applied to the two children she and Philip had at the time, Charles and Anne. "It makes them sound like bastards," Philip grumbled. His husbandly pride was severely dented, and it was to please him that Elizabeth, when Andrew was born later, decided that some of her descendants should have the linked name of Mountbatten-Windsor.

*

That decision was made in 1960, and constitutional experts have argued ever since as to whose name is what. Buckingham Palace refers inquiries on the subject to the Home Office, and the Home Office refers them back to Buckingham Palace. Princess Anne, when she married Mark Phillips, did so in the name of Anne Mountbatten-Windsor. Charles, when he married Diana, did not use a surname at all. He was entered in the marriage register as Charles, Prince of Wales. It remains to be seen whether Andrew will call himself Windsor, Mountbatten-Windsor, or simply Prince Andrew when he marries.

*

Windsor, in fact, was not the original name of Elizabeth's family. Nor is Mountbatten the original name of the relatives from whom Philip borrowed it when he took British citizenship. Both names were assumed in some haste at the height of World War I, when British troops were dying in the thousands on the battlefields of Flanders. As happens during such disasters, their relatives back home looked around for someone to blame. A whispering campaign started against Elizabeth's grandfather, King George V. He was more German than British, people said, and his heart wasn't in the war against Germany. That there was more German than British blood in his veins was true enough. When Queen Anne died two hundred years before, the boorish and bulbous-eyed Elector of Hanover had been invited to Britain to sit on the throne as King George I. His son, George II, grandson Frederick (who died before he could become king), and great-grandson George III all married German princesses. So did that son of George III who was the father of Queen Victoria. Victoria herself was raised so much in the German tradition that the companion of her widowhood, the Scot John Brown—her lover, some think—called her "the wee German lady." Her dead husband had been yet another German, Prince Albert, and their son, King Edward VII, married a Danish princess who was German on her mother's side, while their elder daughter became the mother of Germany's Kaiser Wilhelm. This made him King George V's cousin. To make matters worse, George's wife, Queen Mary, was also German. But George himself, despite all his German blood and German relatives, was stolidly British in thought, word, and deed. He was horrified when he heard what his British subjects were saying about him. If he could hardly do much about his German ancestry or relatives, he could at least trade in his German name of Saxe-Coburg-Gotha. And so he became Windsor. German relatives living in Britain must also adopt British names, he decreed. So his wife's family, the Tecks, became the Cambridges, while the Battenbergs, to which Philip's mother belonged, became the Mountbattens.

*

Diana's name, before she married Charles, was Diana Frances Spencer. Generations ago, in the original Norman-French, the family name was Despencer, signifying a butler.

*

Charles, when he succeeds his mother on the throne, will probably reign as King Charles III. Probably, but not necessarily. Kings and queens pick their own names. Elizabeth has stuck to her own. Her father didn't. In an attempt to stabilize the position of the monarchy in Britain following the shock of his brother's abdication, he decided to revive his father's name. So he was crowned as King George VI though his first name was really Albert and his wife called him "Bertie." Elizabeth's great-grandfather was another Albert who changed his name when he became king, though for a different reason. His mother, Queen Victoria, had made him promise not to use the name he shared with his father, her beloved Prince Albert. So he was crowned King Edward VII.

*

Behind royal backs, palace servants have their own nicknames for members of the family. Like Elizabeth herself, they call Princess Michael "Our Val." Elizabeth's mother is sometimes "the Queen Mum" and sometimes simply "Granny." Charles and Diana's oldest son is "Wee Willie Wales." Prince Andrew, in childhood, was similarly "Andy Pandy," the name of a puppet popular on children's television programs. More recently, "Andy Pandy" has

13

become "Randy Andy" because of his enthusiastic love life. Prince Philip in a bad mood is known as "Annigoni" because of the severe look bestowed on him in a portrait by that painter, while Elizabeth, on a bad day, is similarly styled "Miss Piggy."

*

Before the introduction of numeration to distinguish between monarchs with the same name, they were nearly all tagged with nicknames of one sort or another. Even those over whom there was no confusion were usually given a nickname based on appearance, character, or some personal habit. Thus we have:

> Alfred the Great
> Edward the Elder
> Edgar the Peaceable
> Edward the Martyr
> Ethelred the Unready (which meant "unwise" in Saxon times)
> Edmund Ironside
> Harold Harefoot
> Edward the Confessor
> William the Conqueror
> William Rufus (because he was so red in the face)
> Henry Courtmantle (because of the short cloak he favored)
> Richard the Lionhearted
> John Lackland
> Edward Longshanks (because of his height)

Such nicknames were no longer necessary once numeration came into use. But they still cropped up from time to time when something seized the public fancy. Henry VIII's daughter Mary became "Bloody Mary" because of the hundreds she burned at the stake, while her half-sister Elizabeth, who never married, was "The Virgin Queen." Charles II was "The Merry Monarch" because of his rollicking love life, and Queen Anne was "Brandy Nan" once her subjects got to know of her drinking habits. Elizabeth's great-grandfather, King Edward VII, was nicknamed "Tum-tum" because of his prodigious appetite.

*

The state of Virginia is named after the first Elizabeth, the Virgin Queen. The Carolinas are named for Charles I and Charles II, while Maryland is named after Charles I's wife, Queen Henrietta Maria. New York is named after Charles II's brother, the Duke of York, to whom the King gave the area after the British took it from the Dutch in 1665, and Georgia is named after George II.

*

In attempts, usually unsuccessful, to obtain privacy, members of the royal family not infrequently resort to aliases. This is not a new ploy. It has been going on since Victorian times, at least. Queen Victoria, visiting her royal relatives in Europe, would travel as the Duchess of Balmoral in the hope of obtaining privacy for herself. The Duke of Windsor, in the days when he was King Edward VIII, called himself the Duke of Lancaster while jaunting around the resort spots of the Mediterranean with Mrs. Simpson. For lovey-dovey conversations over the telephone they called each other James and Janet. Princess Margaret, in the days when she was secretly meeting Tony Snowdon, would reserve theater seats and restaurant tables for "Mr. and Mrs. Gordon." Later, when she preferred Roddy Llewellyn to Tony, it became "Mr. and Mrs. Brown" when she and her youthful boyfriend flew out to her holiday home on Mustique. Prince Charles has employed a whole range of aliases. He was "Mr. Postle" when booking a sleeping berth on an overnight train, "Charlie Chester" when joining a club in university days, and "Charles Windsor" when booking a restaurant table in Melbourne, Australia. If one of Diana's flatmates chanced to answer the telephone when he called to date her in their courtship days, he would give his name as "Renfrew." Diana briefly became Deborah Smythson Wells when she went along to try on her wedding dress in secret. She was similarly "Miss Buckingham" for visits to another of her several fashion designers and plain "Mrs. Smith" when she flew from Scotland to London on a British Airways shuttle for a pregnancy test soon after marriage. Returning to Britain from a Caribbean vacation on another British Airways flight, she and Charles booked seats in the name of Hardy. Prince Andrew was "Andrew Edwards" for a three-week stay in France to brush up his French in schooldays and "Andrew Cambridge" for a later trip to Canada, while brother Edward was similarly "Edward Bishop" when vacationing in Italy.

Bloodlines

Geneticists calculate that Charles and Diana's elder son, when he succeeds to Britain's crown as King William V, will be the country's most British monarch since James VI of Scotland rode south to London in 1603 to become James I of England, and also the most American. The blue blood that flows in William's veins, they compute, is made up as follows:

39.375 percent	English
15.625 percent	Scottish
6.25 percent	American
6.25 percent	Irish
32.5 percent	mainly German, but with a dash of Danish and Russian

The American and Irish blood in William's veins comes mainly for his mother. Diana is 25 percent Irish-American. Her American descent is from a seventeenth-century New England farmer named Joseph Morgan. Her great-great-grandfather was Frank Work, a New York millionaire. Much to Work's displeasure, his daughter Frances married an impoverished Irish baronet, James Burke Roche. The marriage failed, but not before Frances had given birth to twin sons, one of them Diana's grandfather, Maurice Burke

Roche. By dint of emerging from his mother's womb twenty minutes ahead of his twin brother, Maurice qualified to inherit his father's title and become the fourth Baron Fermoy. Along with his twin brother, he also qualified to inherit a substantial fortune from his American grandfather on condition that he become a U.S. citizen. This condition, which would have meant surrendering his Irish title, was later quashed by an American court, and Maurice returned to Britain to claim his title with a nest egg of $1.5 million tucked away in his saddlebags. In due course he married a young Scottish concert pianist named Ruth Gill. Their daughter Frances is Diana's mother. As a young concert pianist, Diana's grandmother played duets with a certain Elizabeth Bowes-Lyon, who was to marry the second son of King George V and so become the mother of Queen Elizabeth II. Today, as queen mother, she has Diana's grandmother, Ruth, as lady-in-waiting and counts her among her closest friends.

Diana's descent from Frank Work links her, and William and Henry, with many famous Americans, among them:

> George Washington, America's first president
> The nation's second president, John Adams
> The Roosevelt family
> Calvin Coolidge
> John Pierpont Morgan
> Harriet Beecher Stowe
> Louisa M. Alcott
> Ralph Waldo Emerson
> Gloria Vanderbilt
> Erle Stanley Gardner
> General George Patton
> George Gallup (of Gallup polls fame)
> Nelson Bunker Hunt
> Orson Welles

Humphrey Bogart
Lee Remick

William and Henry also have a smidgen of American ancestry on their father's side. It comes down through Charles' grandmother, that same Elizabeth Bowes-Lyon who is now the queen mother. Just as Diana is descended in part from a New England farmer, Elizabeth's mother is similarly descended in part from a seventeenth-century Virginian, Colonel Augustine Warner. Colonel Warner had two children—a son, also named Augustine, and a daughter, Sarah. Sarah was a great-great-great-grandmother of General Robert E. Lee. Her brother, Augustine, had two daughters, Mildred and Mary. George Washington was Mildred's great-grandson while a great-great-great-great-granddaughter of Mary's married a Scot, Claude Bowes-Lyon, Earl of Strathmore. That was in 1853, and William and Henry are her great-great-grandsons.

*

On their father's side, William and Henry are also descended from the Saxon kings who ruled England before William the Conqueror decided to take the country over in 1066. But there is royal blood on their mother's side, too— even if it comes from the wrong side of the blanket. Two of Diana's ancestresses, the bold and beautiful Lucy Walter and the sensuous and tempestuous Barbara Villiers, were mistresses of that lusty monarch King Charles II, while another, Arabella Churchill, was the mistress of Charles' brother, King James II.

*

Elizabeth and Philip have a somewhat more recent blood tie. Both are great-great-grandchildren of Queen Victoria.

*

19

Diana's forebears on her father's side, if they were never kings, certainly hobnobbed with kings and queens down the centuries. As far back as 1082 a certain Robert Despencer (her family's original name) was one of the barons who counseled William the Conqueror. A sixteenth-century Spencer was knighted by Henry VIII. Another Spencer lent money to King Charles I to pay his troops during England's Civil War while yet another was adviser to no fewer than three kings, Charles II, James II, and William III. By then they were earls, and the daughter of one had King George III as her godfather. The fourth earl held the high office of lord chamberlain, while the fifth served both Queen Victoria and her son, King Edward VII. Diana's father had Queen Mary and the Duke of Windsor as his godparents, and he himself, in his younger days, served as equerry to both Elizabeth and her father before her. Diana's brother and her two sisters all have members of the royal family as godparents. Ironically, Diana herself does not.

*

Like her father-in-law, Prince Philip, Diana is the product of a broken marriage, something which seemed inconceivable in 1954 when her father, accompanying Elizabeth II on her round-the-world tour, begged her to release him from his duties as equerry so that he could fly back to Britain and propose to the beautiful Frances Burke Roche. Their wedding that summer rivaled Elizabeth's own. They were married in Westminster Abbey, where Elizabeth herself had been married a few years before. She and Philip were among the wedding guests. So were Elizabeth's mother and sister, three royal aunts, and two cousins. In all, there were over a thousand guests along with six bridesmaids, three page boys, and a detachment from the Royal Scots Greys forming an honor guard as bride and bridegroom left the ancient abbey. Thirteen years and four children later it was all over, with Frances named as the other woman in a divorce action brought by Janet Shand Kydd. Diana's father then divorced her mother on the grounds of adultery and there was a bitter battle for the custody of the children, which the father won. Frances married the wealthy Peter Shand Kydd and retreated with him to an isolated part of Scotland. Diana was heartbroken, and her tendency to bite her nails stems from that time. There was a further family upset later when Diana's father became involved with the woman who is now her stepmother, the flamboyant Countess of Dartmouth, daughter of that writer of so many love stories, Barbara Cartland. The Earl of Dartmouth divorced his countess, and Diana's father married her. Diana's two elder sisters have never really taken to their stepmother. Diana herself is more tolerant while still remaining close and loyal to her real mother.

*

There was no actual divorce between Prince Philip's parents, but they separated while Philip was still a small boy. His father took off to indulge himself in the fleshpots of Monte Carlo while his mother lived in turn with her four daughters, all of whom had married German princelings. Philip was taken care of by his Mountbatten relatives in England, who also paid for his schooling. As a result of the family split, World War II found Philip serving in the British navy while his brothers-in-law were fighting on the side of Germany.

*

Philip was a baby of only eighteen months, fifth in line of succession to the Greek throne, when his family had to flee into exile. The year was 1922, and Greece was under the heel of a revolutionary junta. Philip's father, Prince Andrew, was arrested and tossed into jail. Others who opposed the new regime had already been summarily executed, and Andrew seemed assured of the same fate. At the risk of her own life, Philip's mother left the family's island home on Corfu and journeyed to Athens in an attempt to save her husband. She appealed for help to her cousin, England's King George V. He dispatched a British secret-service agent, Commander Gerald Talbot, to Athens with instructions to negotiate Prince Andrew's release or, if that failed, to rescue him from prison. Traveling in disguise, Talbot entered Greece on a false passport, bluffed his way into the headquarters of the revolutionary leader, General Pangloss, and demanded Prince Andrew's release. The arrival offshore of a British cruiser, also ordered there by George V, its guns trained on the Greek capital, underlined Talbot's demand. To save face, the Greek revolutionaries were permitted the farce of a court-martial on condition that Prince Andrew would be sentenced only to banishment. After the trial, General Pangloss himself drove Talbot and Philip's father to the quayside to board the British cruiser. With Philip's mother also aboard, the cruiser headed for Corfu to pick up the children. The ship's carpenter obligingly turned an old orange box into an improvised cot for the infant Philip.

*

Charles and Diana's son William was the first royal child in direct line of succession to be born in a proper maternity hospital. His father, Prince Charles, was born at Buckingham Palace, in an outsize bathroom hastily converted to serve as a makeshift delivery room. William's mother, Diana, was born in her mother's bedroom at home. His grandmother, Elizabeth II, was born at the London home of her maternal grandparents. Prince Philip was born in his parents' villa in Corfu—on the dining-room table. Like his own son, Prince Andrew, Philip was a late arrival;

the youngest of his four sisters was seven when he was born. Andrew was an even later arrival; he appeared on the scene—somewhat to his parents' surprise—when Charles was eleven and Anne nine. Elizabeth by then had rather given up any thought of having further children. But Edward, the youngest of Philip and Elizabeth's brood, was a planned baby, conceived as a playmate for Andrew.

*

When William was born Diana was fortunate to escape the embarrassment suffered by earlier royal princesses when producing an heir to the throne. They were obliged to have an official witness present when giving birth. This embarrassing royal custom started with King James II. Aware of his shaky position as a Catholic king in a Protestant country, James crowded the royal bedroom with sixty friends to act as witnesses when his second wife, Mary of Modena, gave birth to a son and heir. In fact, such a large number of witnesses aroused the very suspicions that James was seeking to allay. The rumor spread that the baby was a changeling who had been smuggled into the queen's bed in a warming pan, and James, in due course, lost his crown and was forced to flee the country. After that, Parliament decided to send along its own man to witness future royal births, a practice that continued for Elizabeth's birth in 1926. But things went wrong when Margaret was born four years later. Margaret was born at Glamis Castle in Scotland, and the Home Secretary of the day was deputed to act as witness. He arrived in Scotland far too early and had to be provided with accommodation for the two weeks until the baby was born. This so annoyed the father that, later, when he became King George VI and Elizabeth, in turn, was expecting her first child, he decreed that there was no longer need for such anachronistic nonsense. That ended the whole business, and all Charles had to do when William was born was telephone the Home Secretary and give him the news.

*

William weighed 7 pounds, 1½ ounces at birth and Henry weighed 6 pounds, 14 ounces, which is lighter than either of their parents. Charles weighed in at 7 pounds, 6 ounces and Diana at 7 pounds, 12 ounces.

*

The fresh blood that Elizabeth's mother and now Diana have brought into the royal line has improved the stock. No longer need each new generation fear the birth of a heart-break baby, as was the case when most royals married other royals. Queen Victoria's youngest son, Leopold, was born with hemophilia which left him lame in childhood and caused his death at the age of thirty-one. King Edward VII's eldest son, Albert Victor, was a sickly, backward prince who succumbed to pneumonia only weeks before he was to have been married. King George V's youngest child, John, was an epileptic. His fits were so violent that he was brought up apart from the rest of the family, living with his nanny in an isolated farmhouse where he died at the age of thirteen.

*

Today's royals, by contrast, enjoy robust good health and breed healthy offspring. Elizabeth is no longer troubled by the sinusitis that once plagued her, and it is years since Philip has had an attack of jaundice. His only health problem is a touch of arthritis in the wrist, brought on by too much polo playing in his younger days. Charles has thrown off his tendency to chest colds to which he was subject in childhood, and Diana talks of herself as "a strong, healthy girl" whose only real problem in recent years has been morning sickness in the early stages of pregnancy.

*

For those who believe that character and personality stem from astrological influences, here are the Zodiac signs under which members of the family were born:

Elizabeth II	Taurus
Philip	Gemini
Charles	Scorpio
Diana	Cancer
William	Cancer
Henry	Virgo
Anne	Leo
Mark Phillips	Virgo
Andrew	Aquarius
Edward	Pisces
Queen Mother	Leo
Margaret	Leo

Elizabeth II has two birthdays each year, her real one on April 21 and an official one on a variable date in June. Like so many royal traditions, the dual birthday custom started with Queen Victoria. Parliament wanted her birthday to be a day of public celebration with the queen parading through the streets of London. But Victoria preferred to spend her birthday quietly at home with her husband and children. So Parliament had to be content with another date, and today what is known as the Queen's Birthday Parade, a colorful display of military pageantry, is usually held on the second Saturday in June. June is selected because it gives a reasonable chance of fine weather while a Saturday means that London's streets are not choked with working-week traffic.

*

Elizabeth's aunt, Princess Alice, and one of her cousins, Princess Alexandra, both celebrate their birthdays on

25

Christmas Day. "The only nice thing to happen this year," said Elizabeth's grandmother, Queen Mary, when Alexandra was born. It was 1936, the year the Duke of Windsor abdicated. While Alexandra has to celebrate both Christmas and her birthday on December 25, her son, James, is in an even worse fix. He was born on February 29, 1964, which means a birthday only once every four years.

Other royal birthdates are:

Philip	June 10, 1921
Charles	November 14, 1948
Diana	July 1, 1961
William	June 21, 1982
Henry	September 15, 1984
Andrew	February 19, 1960
Edward	March 10, 1964
Anne	August 15, 1950
Mark	September 22, 1948
Queen Mother	August 4, 1900
Margaret	August 21, 1930

*

Almost from the moment he was old enough to understand, William has had the royal tradition of politeness and good manners drilled into him, and the same will apply to his younger brother, Henry. Their parents' aim, Charles says, is "to bring up our children to be good-mannered, to think of other people, to do unto others as they would have done unto them." It is a maxim Charles himself learned at his mother's knee and his mother at her mother's knee. "Royalty is no excuse for bad manners," Elizabeth's mother drilled into her. Once, overhearing her daughter address the man who came to wind the palace clocks only by his surname, she made her go back and apologize. "I'm sorry I didn't 'mister' you," the young Elizabeth told him. In turn, she drilled the same lesson into her own children. Charles and Anne, in childhood, were made to say "please" and "thank you" so much that they even said "please" when dispatching a corgi to retrieve a ball and "thank you" when the ball was brought back.

Purely Personal

Elizabeth likes horses and dogs, deer stalking, walking in the rain, Scottish dancing, military bands, the novels of Dick Francis, crossword puzzles, tweeds, China tea, fresh fruit salad, cream cheese, mint chocolates, Chinese gooseberries, and carnations (her favorite flower).

She does not like caviar, oysters, grouse, escargot, cats, garlic, heights, loud noises, or unpunctuality.

Horses are her great passion. Her favorite reading in childhood was *Black Beauty*. Today it is a massive tome titled *Family Tables of Racehorses* which lists the pedigrees of over 40,000 thoroughbreds. People less enthusiastic about horses might find such reading boring, but Elizabeth classes it as "completely absorbing."

Her secret ambition is to breed a horse that will win the Derby, Britain's most prestigious race. Her horses have won scores of other races over the years, among them the Oaks and St. Leger in Britain and the Prix de Diane in France, but the Derby has so far eluded her. She stores her racing and breeding data on a computer given to her by President Reagan when she visited his California ranch in 1983, and a recent ploy, in pursuit of that elusive Derby winner, has been to ship some of her mares to Kentucky for mating with American stallions.

Though she breeds and races horses, Elizabeth never

bets. Nor does she any longer give racing tips to friends and servants. That stopped the time she told her page that one of her horses was a surefire winner. He had a $3 bet on it—and lost.

*

Philip, on the other hand, finds horse racing an utter bore. When obliged to accompany Elizabeth to such horse racing occasions as Royal Ascot, he invariably retreats to the room at the rear of the royal box and whiles away the time watching cricket on television. He also dislikes modern art, red wine, time wasted sipping afternoon tea and nibbling cucumber sandwiches, press photographers, smoky rooms, and people who cough or sneeze in his vicinity, and he is inclined to be suspicious of anyone who keeps tropical fish. "Be very, very careful of people who have tropical fish in their homes," he told a 1984 news conference in Washington. "Such people are usually suffering from some psychiatric problem."

He likes painting in oils, photographing wild birds, carriage driving, white wine, escargot, mustard with his roast beef, beer drunk from a pewter tankard, prefers a shower to a bath, and likes to stretch out at night in a really big bed. Staying at the White House he certainly got one—the massive 97-inch bed with a horsehair mattress that Mrs. Lincoln bought for husband, Abe.

*

Diana likes brown bread, borscht, lemon soufflé and homemade fudge; taking photographs of her children; the Muppets; playing bridge; the novels of Daphne du Maurier, Mary Stewart, and her step-grandmother, Barbara Cartland; tap dancing; ballet; and skiing. She does not like riding, swimming in the sea, washing up, being pregnant—"If men had to have babies," she says, "they would only have one each"—or eavesdropping journalists, and is not exactly enamored of her husband's hunting and shooting exploits.

*

Charles likes fox hunting and fishing, playing polo, music (especially Bach, Beethoven, and Mozart, the Three Degrees, and the Beatles), bread-and-butter pudding, uglis (an exotic fruit that he enjoys for breakfast), gin and tonic, lace-up shoes, self-supporting trousers, and old lavatory seats (he collects them). He does not like red wine, waistcoats, the smell of paint, people who think George III was mad, modern architecture, or books and games that "appeal to the black side of children."

Given a book called *Ghastly Games* to take home to William when he attended the 1984 British Book Production Awards, he skimmed through it and said bluntly, "I think these are terrible. They are all horrible games."

Nor has he so far been persuaded to become a Freemason, though his father and one of his cousins, the Duke of Kent, are members, as were his grandfather, King George VI, and his great-uncle, the Duke of Windsor.

*

Andrew likes parachuting and mountaineering, actresses, beauty queens, and female models, photography, books on history, and the music of Genesis and Pink Floyd. He does not like polo, reading fiction, watching television (though he was something of an addict in childhood), classical music, or the red-carpet treatment he gets wherever he goes. Indeed, he sometimes wishes he weren't a royal prince, he has said. In his view, the responsibilities outweigh the privileges.

*

Anne likes horses, fast driving, horses, TV westerns, horses, and more horses. She does not like press photo-

31

graphers, being pregnant, or watching soccer (a spectacle husband Mark thoroughly enjoys).

*

Elizabeth's mother likes open windows, log fires, playing solitaire, crinolines, chocolates, green grapes, champagne cocktails, steeplechases, reading whodunnits, and having breakfast in bed. She does not like romantic fiction, clock watchers, or stuffy rooms and has never had any great love for the Duchess of Windsor.

*

The royals are a family of hidden talents. Diana is a *Cordon Bleu* cook and a tap dancer of no mean ability. She tried to teach Charles to tap dance, but he quickly called it a day. "It's too hard on my poor feet," he groaned. In addition to his better-known hunting, shooting, and fishing exploits, he is also a writer, painter, and musician. A children's book he wrote for his brothers when they were small, *The Old Man of Lochnagar*, became a bestseller. He plays the cello, though he lacks practice, and two of his paintings, watercolors executed while he was on honeymoon with Diana, were exhibited in London not long ago.

*

His father, Philip, prefers to paint in oils. "A simple style … a lot of promise," one art critic has said of his efforts, but Elizabeth, who herself knows a lot about art, liked one of her husband's paintings sufficiently to hang it in their private sitting room at Windsor Castle. Anne and Charles also have examples of their father's artwork hanging in their respective homes. Philip has given paintings to one or two close friends, but only the friends know who the artist is. The last thing Philip wants is for his paintings to find their way into auction rooms and sell for unrealistic prices because he is who he is. So, modestly, he does not sign them.

32

Philip is also a photographer, model maker, designer, and inventor of no mean ability. He has had a book of photographs published under the title *Birds from Britannia*. He once built a scale model of Balmoral Castle, the family's Scottish residence, complete to the smallest detail. Impatient with the necessity of wriggling in and out of tight-fitting breeches in his polo-playing days, he invented a quick-change pair with a zipper running down each leg. (Incidentally, his uncle, the late Earl Mountbatten, is credited with being the first man to have trousers made with a zipper instead of buttons.) Philip also designed one of Elizabeth's favorite bracelets, the swivel kettle she uses when making tea, the plastic bubble fitted to the royal car in Canada so that she could still be clearly seen in bad weather, and the bronze fountain that stands in the rose garden at Windsor.

*

Elizabeth's mother is an expert and experienced salmon fisher, knows how to use a handgun (she learned in wartime when a German invasion of Britain seemed imminent), and has a repertoire of magic tricks with which to amuse her great-grandchildren. She can also recite "The Shooting of Dan McGrew" by heart, and when President Reagan had dinner at Buckingham Palace during his 1984 visit to Britain for the London economic summit, the two of them vied with each other as to who could recite it better.

Elizabeth herself is a crack shot with a hunting rifle and has numerous stags to her credit. She could also overhaul her car if necessary. She learned how during her wartime stint in the Auxiliary Territorial Service.

*

Princess Anne is one of comparatively few women in Britain qualified to drive heavy-goods vehicles. Visiting

33

British troops in Germany on one occasion, she even took over the controls of a 52-ton Chieftain tank. She also displayed an aptitude with a submachine gun that would have done credit to a James Bond girl, scoring eleven bulls-eyes in a burst of twenty rounds. Princess Margaret, her friends say, could have been a musical-comedy star if she had not been born a princess. She can often be heard vocalizing in the bath, and at one birthday party she delighted the rest of the family with a rip-roaring impersonation of Sophie Tucker. Elizabeth can sing, too, and at Christmas parties she and Margaret will sometimes join forces in a duet. "You're Just in Love" from *Call Me Madam* and "The Rain in Spain" from *My Fair Lady* are two of their favorites.

*

On two things Elizabeth is an acknowledged expert—paintings and racehorses. Shortly after succeeding to the throne she made a tour of the immense collection of paintings that was among her royal inheritance. She paused in front of two that were listed as the work of Rubens. "I don't think those are by Rubens," she said, and subsequent investigation proved her correct. The same—despite the wrong racing tip she once gave her page—with racehorses. She was at a race meeting when someone suggested that a particular horse was a certain winner. Elizabeth did not agree. "Its sire and its dam were both sprinters," she said. "It can't possibly win over a mile and a quarter." Nor did it. It is said that she can reel off the pedigree of every royal racehorse right back to Eclipse (which was bred in George II's day). Certainly, Australians sent out a panic call when she went racing there on one occasion: "For heaven's sake, get someone to the royal box who really knows the form and the stud book. Her Majesty has it all off pat."

*

Elizabeth likes an old-fashioned Christmas with all her family around her, sons and daughter-in-law, daughter and son-in-law, grandchildren, her mother and sister along with her sister's children, her cousins and their children—a family party of over thirty all told. So that all except the very youngest (like William, Henry, and Anne's two children) are free to go to church with her on Christmas morning, Elizabeth insists that grown-ups in the party give each other their gifts on Christmas Eve. With some thirty people giving and receiving presents, it could be chaos if things were not properly organized. So trestle tables are set in line near a giant Christmas tree. The tables are divided into sections with colored ribbon. Each section is labeled with the name of a member of the family so that the others know where to pile their presents.

*

Just as Elizabeth made and filled Christmas stockings for her own children when they were small, so she now makes and fills them for her grandchildren. She prefers her own to those bought in the shops. She also makes a Christmas stocking for each of her pet corgis, filling them with a doggy selection of chocolate drops, dog biscuits, a rubber ball, and a chewy imitation bone.

*

The royal family's favorite party game is charades. A big box of fancy costumes and props enables them to play the game in style, dressing up as maids, waiters, huntsmen, vamps of the 1920s, or whatever else takes their fancy. Most of them are ham actors at heart. Charles, in schooldays, played the title role in Shakespeare's *Macbeth*. Philip, a generation before, was an armed warrior in the same schoolboy production. Andrew, during schooldays in Canada, acted in the musical *Oliver!,* and Edward, during his time in New Zealand, took part in a school production

35

of *Charley's Aunt*. Anne, in schooldays, took a boy's part in Christopher Fry's play, *The Boy with a Cart*. Even Elizabeth has acted in her time. At the age of sixteen, wearing a short tunic and silk tights that revealed shapely legs, she played the title role in an amateur production of *Aladdin and His Wonderful Lamp*. Margaret was also in the show, and years later, while she was married to Tony Snowdon, played Queen Victoria in a private movie produced by Peter Sellers. Snowdon and Brit Ekland were also in the film.

*

Royal games of charades are also enlivened by the fact that Elizabeth, Diana, Margaret, and Anne are all excellent mimics. Diana's favorite piece of mimicry is Miss Piggy. Anne is good at taking off some of Britain's top politicians. Margaret can impersonate a wide variety of famous singers, among them Bing Crosby and Sophie Tucker. Elizabeth has a whole range of accents on call—Scots, Irish, American—and her imitation of a London Cockney has to be heard to be believed. Tired after a long day of official engagements culminating in a royal banquet, she whipped off her shoes and tiara on her way back to her own apartment. Shoes in one hand, tiara in the other, she rounded a corner and almost bumped into one of the servants. Unabashed, she promptly pretended to hobble. "Oo-er, me poo-er achin' back," she wailed in a whining Cockney accent. She has done her Cockney impersonation so often she sometimes lapses into it without thinking, as on the occasion when it began to rain as she crossed the courtyard toward her car. "Cor lumme if it ain't bloomin' raining and I ain't got me brolly," she exclaimed. (A "brolly," in Cockney, is an umbrella.)

*

A quieter diversion that Elizabeth prefers when she has friends to dinner is the name game. Dinner guests are given the names of the sire and dam of a thoroughbred foal Elizabeth has bred and invited to suggest an appropriate name. Several of her royal racehorses have been named as a result of the game—Stenographer (out of Saucy Lass by Fair Copy), Pall Mall (Malapert–Palestine), Prairie Song (Open Country–Pinza), Royal Taste (Kingstone–Saucy Lass) and Rosy Glow (Borealis–Terracotta), for example.

*

Like everyone else, the royals have their weaknesses. Elizabeth can be obstinate. Her mother is notoriously unpunctual. Nor is Diana always the best of timekeepers. Diana also bites her nails. Charles can be dilatory and Andrew arrogant. Anne has a jealous streak. Philip can be both tetchy and vain. Nearsighted as he is, he has had to wear glasses for years, but contrives to conceal the fact by keeping them carefully tucked in his pocket until he is away from the crowds. Elizabeth has no such option. She can no longer read without glasses and must don them openly in order to see her notes when making a speech.

*

Where punctuality is concerned, Elizabeth and her mother are complete opposites. Like her father and grandfather before her, Elizabeth II considers punctuality a virtue of the highest order. Invariably on time herself, she expects the same of others. Her aides have learned to watch for a trick of flipping her engagement ring around and around on her finger. It is a sure sign that someone or something is running late and she doesn't like it.

Her mother, on the other hand, is often unpunctual, a trait that was the despair of her husband in the days when they were king and queen. With an official engagement in the offing, he would be ready on the dot—then be forced to wait anything up to fifteen minutes for his wife, pacing impatiently up and down, consulting his watch, twisting his signet ring around and around on his finger (as Elizabeth does with her engagement ring). She was so late one evening when they were due at the Royal Opera House that he told a footman, "Kindly inform the queen that I am leaving without her." Just at that moment, however, Elizabeth's mother put in a belated appearance, resplendent in tiara and crinoline. "Well, are we all ready?" she inquired blithely.

*

Since becoming queen, the daughter has devised a method of ensuring that her mother turns up at palace dinner parties on time. She sends word to her that dinner is being served half an hour earlier than is actually the case.

*

The royals, these days, are a close-knit family, supportive of each other. It is well known that the British government makes an annual allowance to three of Elizabeth's cousins—the Duke of Gloucester, the Duke of Kent, and his sister, Princess Alexandra—to help them live in a style befitting princes and a princess. Less well known is the fact that this money comes indirectly from Elizabeth. She reimburses the government out of her private income. Philip, on a more modest scale, has similarly helped his sisters in Germany from time to time. And when his aging mother was taken ill in Germany, he flew out there to bring her back to London and arranged her admission to a hospital. The last few years of her life were spent at Buckingham Palace, looked after by her royal daughter-in-law.

*

The royals were not always such a close-knit, devoted family. Queen Victoria and her eldest son, later King

Edward VII, were continually at loggerheads. Edward, in turn, though a doting father, was an unfaithful husband who had many mistresses. Elizabeth's grandfather, King George V, by contrast, was a faithful husband but a martinet of a father whose children had to make appointments to see him. "My father was frightened of his mother," he used to say. "I was frightened of my father, and I'm damned well going to see to it that my children are frightened of me." It was almost certainly fear of his father that gave Elizabeth's father his lifelong stammer.

*

More than anyone, it was Elizabeth's mother who turned the royals from the divided family they were into the united family of today. When her brother-in-law abdicated and her husband unexpectedly became king, she proved herself a loyal and supportive wife, encouraging him to bring in a speech therapist to help control his stammer, persuading him to take up gardening as an antidote to the stress and strain of kingship. She had their private rooms at Buckingham Palace redecorated in brighter, more cheerful colors, filled the place with flowers, saw to it that royal menus included his favorite dishes, and ended the long-standing royal tradition that king and queen must eat apart from their children. The family would all eat together, she insisted.

*

"I have been trained never to show emotion in public," says Elizabeth II. It was her grandmother, Queen Mary, not her mother, who instilled that into her. But in private Elizabeth can be as emotive as the next person. She will let out a loud peal of laughter if something amuses her, has been known to scream during a horror movie, and can whoop as loudly as anyone when indulging in Scottish dancing. Even in public her emotions can sometimes get the

39

better of her. She was obliged to blink away tears as she
drove to Westminster Abbey for her coronation and again
in Australia when the then prime minister, John Menzies,
welcomed her with the words: "You are in your own
country, among your own people. We are all yours—all
parties, all creeds."

Her private sitting room at the palace is crowded with
sentimentally treasured photographs of her dead father, of
Philip in the days when she first knew him, of the two of
them on their honeymoon, of Charles, Anne, Andrew, and
Edward as babies. She works at the same desk her father
did, sits at it on a chair needleworked by her grandmother.
She hoards keepsakes—a silver-backed hairbrush she had as
a child, a rope of pearls her grandparents gave her when she
was nine, a recording of "People Will Say We're in Love"
that Philip gave her in courtship days, and a baby's rattle
with Charles' teething marks on it.

*

As well as being sentimental, Elizabeth is a mite superstitious. If she spills salt, she will throw some over her
shoulder to ward off bad luck. She is equally quick to
separate crossed knives and so prevent a quarrel. If a
candle on the royal dining table goes out, she thinks it is
inviting bad luck to relight it with a fresh match. But bad
luck becomes good luck if a taper is used to relight it from
one of the other candles. Bad luck can also ensue, she
believes, if thirteen people sit together at dinner. Royal
aides are aware of Elizabeth's superstitious regard for the
number thirteen and, on the rare occasion when the total for
dinner is thirteen, a lady-in-waiting or equerry will tact-
fully offer to withdraw. There was one occasion, however,
when this was not possible. There were already twelve for
dinner, either relatives or VIPs, when Prince Charles
turned up unexpectedly. Elizabeth promptly gave instruc-

tions for two tables to be pushed apart so that the dinner party would be split into two groups. A single large tablecloth covered both tables, disguising what had been done.

*

At New Year Elizabeth still observes the ancient custom known as "first footing." The tallest and darkest among her pages and footmen is deputed to be the "tall dark stranger" who enters promptly on the stroke of midnight bearing gifts for the ladies of the family. The "gifts" take the form of potted plants and small pieces of coal, modern versions of the wild plants and firewood favored by Elizabeth's Saxon ancestors.

*

In disposition, Elizabeth II takes more after her father than her mother. But her temper does not flare as his sometimes did. It is many years since she actually lost her temper. It happened at a private dance in the days when she was a young princess. Suddenly she abandoned her dancing partner, a young army officer, stalked off the floor, sent for her coat, sent for her car, and returned abruptly to her palace home. "I've never been so humiliated," she snapped. "Horsey, indeed."

These days, if someone offends her, she says nothing, but merely freezes them with an icy stare that, her aides joke, can kill at ten paces. Even Philip was once known to dry up in the middle of a good story when he found his wife's disapproving stare focused in his direction.

*

Philip, by contrast, is a man whose temper has a short fuse, a prince who does not suffer fools gladly and resents criticism. Adverse comment about himself or another of the family in one of Britain's newspapers can spark him into thumping the nearest item of furniture with his fist and letting out a roar of "Bloody fool!" *Bloody* is his favorite swearword, press photographers his pet hate. "Bloody lousy photographers," he called them in Sweden, "vultures" in Australia. Two photographers once accused him of dowsing them with a water spray at a London flower show. In Pakistan, spying a photographer who had scaled a pole in the hope of getting a better shot, Philip snorted, "I hope he breaks his bloody neck." "Pee off," he told another photographer in Canada. In Brazil he may have said something even stronger to a photographer trotting alongside the royal car. A reporter who lip-read the remark was so surprised he sought confirmation from a royal aide. "I think Prince Philip was speaking French," said the aide, diplomatically. Elizabeth, reading this later in a newspaper, could not restrain a smile. "I didn't know Prince Philip could speak French," she said slyly.

Philip's long-standing abhorrence of photographers stems from an evening not long before Charles was born. Philip and Elizabeth had been out to dine with his Mountbatten relatives. It was dark as they drove back to the palace, Philip at the wheel. Photographers were lying in wait outside the palace, hoping to get yet another picture of the young royal mother-to-be. Momentarily blinded by the glare of flashbulbs, Philip swerved, and the car nearly crashed into one of the massive stone pillars supporting the palace gates. "Bloody fools," he stormed as he helped Elizabeth from the car. "We could have been killed."

*

Philip's antipathy toward press photographers does not extend to newspaper cartoonists. Even insulting cartoons of himself make him chuckle, and publication is usually followed by a telephone call from the palace. Not to reprimand the editor, but to ask if Philip can have the original. By now, he has quite a collection hanging in his rooms at Sandringham.

*

Charles has a much more phlegmatic disposition than his father. Even so, photographers' calls of "Look this way" have been known to irritate. "I'm not a horse," he snapped back on one occasion. But, as with his mother, it is years since he's been known to lose his temper. The occasion was a polo game in Nassau. The commentator's rather labored jokes about Charles and his parents became an increasing source of irritation as the game progressed. Finally Charles could stand it no more. He dismounted and, red in the face with anger, pounded up the steps of the commentary box. "This is supposed to be a polo game," he barked. "You're turning it into a barn dance."

Diana, similarly, came close to losing her temper during the couple's 1983 tour of Canada. Cause of her displeasure was an attempt to sneak a microphone between people's legs to eavesdrop on what she was saying. "Do that again and I'll kick it," she threatened.

*

Of all the royal children, Anne is most like Philip. Like him, she does not suffer fools gladly. Like him, she speaks her piece. "Bloody wind," she muttered in Australia when her hair blew in her eyes. "Silly bastard," she snapped when husband Mark came a cropper in an equestrian event, though whether she was referring to Mark or his horse was unclear. But it was clearly Mark she was angry with at another riding event, in Germany. Upset by his friendliness with one of the girl grooms, she flung him a souvenir T-shirt with which she had been presented. "You can give that to your stable girl," she sniffed.

*

Anne is a no-nonsense person who revels in fast driving. Several times the police have caught her speeding. Twice she was let off with a caution, but a third time she was fined the equivalent of $60.

She is determined, too. In 1971, following a spell in the hospital, she found herself left out of the British team for the European Eventing Championship. Her pride hurt, she entered on her own account. Hands and legs alike had gone flabby while in the hospital. Aboard the royal yacht, as it took the family north to Balmoral that summer, she played endless games of deck tennis to harden her hands. In Scotland, to strengthen her legs, she trotted briskly up and down mountains. All that, plus taking a couple of risky shortcuts in the actual event, saw her win the championship, beating not only Britain's official team from which she had been omitted but also the top riders from Russia, Italy, France, and Ireland.

*

Most of the royal family are fresh-air fiends, outdoor people. In London, Elizabeth takes a brisk daily walk in the forty-acre garden at the rear of her palace. At Windsor Castle, where she spends her weekends, she goes riding. At her country homes, Sandringham and Balmoral, she walks miles every day with her dogs whatever the weather, striding out across fields and moors in stout shoes, tweeds, a kerchief, plus an added raincoat if it is raining.

Philip and Charles, similarly, are never happier than when they are out and about in the open, up and doing. "Ten minutes' doing is worth ten hours' watching," says Philip. Charles says, "If I wasn't who I am, I would love to have been a farmer." Denied this, he once took off secretly to spend a week working on a small farm, milking cows, spreading muck, and helping to bring a calf into the world.

*

Despite her own country upbringing, Diana is less responsive to the call of the great outdoors. In particular, she has been nervous of horses from the age of nine, when she was thrown and broke an arm. Charles persuaded her to try riding again shortly after they were married, but she was relieved when pregnancy intervened to prevent her from going on with it, and she has not ridden again since.

To please Charles, she also went deer stalking with him when they were in Scotland following their honeymoon and was even persuaded to try her skill with his hunting rifle. But the act of shooting a deer so horrified her that she has never repeated the experience and subsequently rebelled over going with him when he went pheasant shooting, as her royal mother-in-law always goes with Philip.

Diana abhors the thought of killing for sport and, wifelike, worries about Charles when he goes fox hunting, as well she might. He has a record of spills. Since their return from Canada in 1983 there are signs that her attitude has begun to rub off on her husband. While he went out with the stalking parties as usual during their vacation at Balmoral that summer, he himself did no actual shooting. Nor, that fall, did he go pheasant shooting at Sandringham, though Philip did. And he has cut down considerably on his fox-hunting forays.

*

Diana's secret dream in schooldays was to be a ballet dancer. "But I grew too tall," she laments. The nearest she came to realizing that schoolgirl dream was a brief spell teaching small children the rudiments of ballet, though she never actually qualified as a ballet teacher. But if you can't be a ballet dancer yourself, the next best thing is to have your own ballet company. Since 1983 Diana has been the royal patron of the London City Ballet, a small, struggling company existing on a financial shoestring, though her

45

patronage has already helped toward changing that state of affairs.

*

Four of the royal family—Philip, Charles, Andrew, and Elizabeth's cousin, Prince Michael of Kent—are qualified pilots. Edward is expected to join the group shortly and, indeed, may already have done so by the time this book is published. Charles, before marriage, did a stint as a naval helicopter pilot, and Andrew is currently serving in the same capacity—which is a far cry from the days when Philip first flew a helicopter. Winston Churchill was so horrified when he heard (helicopters were regarded as dangerous in those days) that he demanded of Philip's principal aide, Mike Parker: "Is it the intention to wipe out the royal family in the shortest possible time?"

Philip's enthusiasm for flying was born of frustration in the early years of Elizabeth's monarchy. Having resigned his navy job to play the part of royal consort, he found himself with almost nothing to do. At least nothing he regarded as meaningful. So he decided to learn to fly. A Royal Air Force flight lieutenant, Caryl Gordon, was given the task of teaching him. "If you kill him," Gordon was told, "you realize what that will do to the queen." That was in 1952. In the years since, Philip has flown everything from Chipmunk and Harvard trainers to Meteors and Vampires, helicopters and flying boats, Boeings and Tridents, the aging Andovers of what is known as "the Queen's Flight" and, of course, the Concorde.

*

Philip, in his sixties, is no longer the trigger-happy man he used to be, though he still bags his fair share of pheasants and grouse on the royal estates. Time was when he shot anything and everything, not only pheasants and grouse, but deer in Scotland, wild duck in Canada and Italy, wild pig in Holland, boar in Germany, mountain goat in Pakistan, crocodiles in Australia, and a tiger in India. A man who cannot sit still, who does not know how to relax, he has tried most forms of sport in his time—cricket, rugby, boxing, hockey, athletics, yachting, swimming, fishing, shooting, deer stalking, wildfowling, gliding, falconry, big-game hunting, water skiing, spear fishing, polo, and skittles. He even tried golf in his early days but quickly gave it up as "too tame" and settled for polo instead. Since arthritis in his wrist forced him to give up polo, he has taken up carriage driving, and it is largely due to his interest and influence that there is now a world carriage-driving championship. His ambition is to get the sport included in the Olympics, but so far his overtures in this direction have met with no success.

*

Polo players are rated on a scale of two to ten, according to ability. Philip at his peak had a rating of 5. Charles, a less aggressive player than his father, has so far gotten no higher than 4. Andrew doesn't like polo. After two sessions of professional tuition, he decided that the game wasn't for him and gave it up.

*

Time was when Philip would go anywhere, do anything, for a game of polo. He once found himself accompanying Elizabeth on a visit to Holy Island, off Britain's northeast coast, on the day his team was playing in the final of the Royal Windsor Cup. An intricate combination of high-speed launch, naval destroyer, airplane, and two fast cars enabled him to slip away from the tour and cover the 330 miles to Windsor in time to score two of his side's seven match-winning goals.

*

47

Enthusiasm for polo has seen Philip at varying times limping around with a broken ankle, nursing a torn thigh muscle, and having one arm in a sling. But it was yachting, not polo, that nearly cost him his life. His yacht capsized in rough weather and had to be towed in. Philip, standing right beneath the crane, was watching the yacht being towed up the slipway when the crane snapped. Philip looked up and sprang aside in the nick of time as thirty feet of steelwork crashed on the spot he had been occupying a split second before.

*

Elizabeth, in her early days as queen, had an equally narrow escape. She was out riding with others of the royal family at Windsor. Their ride took them in the direction of Ascot racetrack, and a quiet canter suddenly turned into a competitive hell-for-leather gallop to the winning post. Elizabeth was riding flat out when there was a sudden shout of "Look out, Your Majesty!" from a watching workman. She looked up to see a broken cable dangling across the track and flattened herself along her horse just in time to prevent being hurled from the saddle.

*

Charles and Anne have both broken their noses at different times. Anne broke hers when her horse threw her. Charles broke his playing rugby in schooldays. Spills while steeplechasing, fox hunting, and playing polo have brought bumps and bruises galore in more recent times, and there was one polo game in Florida when he collapsed with heat exhaustion. Charles himself firmly believes that his life was saved on that occasion by a royal aide named Oliver Everett. It was Everett who applied cold towels to Charles' body before he was rushed to the hospital.

*

Apart from her family, horses and dogs are the two great loves of Elizabeth's life. No dog or horse has ever been known to frighten her. Her sister, Princess Margaret, once owned a Sealyham that turned out to be a snarler and a snapper. Royal servants gave it a wide berth as it stood guard at the door of Margaret's room. But not Elizabeth. She marched straight up to it whenever she wanted to see her sister. Ignoring its snarls and eluding its snapping teeth, she would take it by the scruff of the neck and lift it aside, saying, "Out, you."

She was the same with a fiery stallion sent to her as a gift from the Russians. "It was enormous," a former royal aide remembers. "It frightened you just to look at it. I personally wouldn't have gone anywhere near the brute." But Elizabeth strode resolutely toward it as it stamped and snorted in the stable yard at Windsor, dodged its snapping teeth, swung herself into the saddle, took a firm grip on the reins, and proceeded to teach it who was queen.

*

Elizabeth's favorite dogs are corgis and Labradors. Because their boisterous romping would wreak havoc among the priceless antiques at Buckingham Palace, Elizabeth has the Labradors with her only in the country, at Balmoral and Sandringham. But the corgis have the run of the palace, scampering into the royal bedroom first thing in the morning, dashing ahead of their royal mistress as she greets luncheon guests, lying under the table at mealtimes (where Elizabeth surreptitiously feeds them an occasional titbit).

Not all the royal corgis, however, are pedigree dogs. Some are what Elizabeth refers to as "dorgis," her nickname for the offspring of a romantic encounter between one of her own corgis and a dachshund belonging to sister Margaret.

Elizabeth's first-ever corgi, given to her in childhood, was named Dookie. Later came Susan, Sugar, Jane and Honey, Whisky and Sherry (which were the childhood pets of Charles and Anne), Heather, Buzz, Foxy, and Tiny. More recent names include Smoky, Shadow, Spark, Myth, Fable, Diamond, Piper, and Chipper.

Royal servants detest the snappy little creatures. Elizabeth adores them and, if she is around, always insists on personally feeding them. The result is a quaint royal ritual. Promptly at five o'clock each afternoon a footman bearing a tray makes his way along the red-carpeted corridor that flanks the royal apartment. On the tray reposes a bag of dog biscuits, a tureen of hot gravy, a supply of cooked meat, and a spoon and fork, both solid silver. The tray is set down on a side table near the door of the royal sitting room. A moment later Elizabeth emerges from the sitting room, corgis and dorgis in close attendance. Using the silver spoon and fork, she mixes the biscuit and meat, pours on the hot gravy, then doles the mixture into a series of bowls, one for each dog.

*

During holidays at Balmoral and Sandringham she will walk for miles with the dogs racing and chasing back and forth around her. There was one occasion when a visitor to Balmoral, playing a round of golf on the private nine-hole course there, was disturbed in midswing by a piercing whistle and topped his shot. He was about to express his feelings in golfing vernacular when he realized that the whistle had come from his royal hostess. Elizabeth, if her dogs stray, calls them back with a fingers-in-mouth whistle. She learned the knack from Philip, who says he perfected it "the hard way—getting taxis in London's wartime blackout."

*

It was at Sandringham, on another occasion, that Elizabeth took her dogs ratting ... and lost her wristwatch in the process. It was a very special watch, a childhood gift from France, made from platinum, adorned with diamonds, and reputed to be the smallest watch in the world. With the help of farm workers, she searched for the watch until it was too dark to search anymore. Over the course of the next week, royal servants and boy scouts also hunted for it. So did soldiers equipped with mine detectors. It was never found. Gallantly and generously, however, the French later had an exact replica made, which she still wears.

*

There was another occasion, also at Sandringham, when one of the dogs was lost. News of its loss was given to Elizabeth while she was eating dinner. The meal over, she put a coat on over her evening dress, took a flashlight and went out in the dark to look for the missing dog. It was midwinter, bitterly cold, with snow on the ground. She heard yelping in the darkness, traced the noise to its source, and found the dog trapped in a thornbush. Oblivious to the damage to her evening dress, she crouched in the snow, pulling and tugging at the prickly undergrowth until the dog was free.

A la Carte

With two exceptions—Elizabeth's mother and her sister, Margaret—the royals are all weight watchers. With good reason. If they were not, the number of luncheons, dinners, and banquets they are obliged to attend in the course of the royal round would soon see them all rolling around like a load of Christmas puddings.

Gluttony has been the deadly sin of many past kings and queens. Queen Anne was so fat she could not stand at her coronation. George IV became so corpulent that the elegant Beau Brummel would refer to him as "my fat friend." Elizabeth's great-grandfather, King Edward VII, changed in a very few years from a slender and handsome prince to a portly one measuring 44 inches around his midriff. "Tum-tum," his friends nicknamed him.

Edward VII had a prodigious appetite. He would wolf his way through a plate heaped with bacon and eggs followed by fish followed by woodcock. And that was simply his breakfast. Four other meals—lunch, afternoon tea, dinner, and supper—followed in the course of the day. Dinner was a gargantuan repast, running as often as not to eight or ten dishes. Caviar would be followed by turtle soup and turtle soup by oysters. Then would come eggs in aspic, pigeon pie, snipe stuffed with foie gras, woodcock stuffed with truffles, ortolans steeped in brandy, and something sweet to

53

end. Even that lot was not enough to satisfy the inner king, and he would have a servant bring a mid-morning snack to keep him going between breakfast and lunch or order a plate of sandwiches if he stayed up gambling into the early hours of the morning.

*

Today's royals, by contrast, are modest eaters. Elizabeth always has been. Philip was a big eater in boyhood, even to clearing his sisters' plates, but nowadays, like Elizabeth, he eats more sparingly, and more quickly too. He is the fastest eater in the royal family, servants say. In San Francisco Philip was served roast beef. He asked for mustard to go with it. The mustard arrived quickly enough, but the beef had already gone.

*

Elizabeth prefers plain food in the English tradition. Philip's tastes are only slightly more exotic, though he drew the line when the New York–based Explorers Club included hippopotamus steaks, lionburgers, and roast buffalo in the menu for its annual dinner. Philip declined to attend and resigned his club membership. He was "appalled by the exhibition of bad taste," he said.

*

Neither Philip nor Elizabeth has cereal or porridge at breakfast. At dinner, delicacies like caviar, oysters, and pheasant are conspicuous only in their absence. Pies, puddings, and cakes are never seen on the dining table. In effect, both Philip and Elizabeth restrict themselves to a high-protein, low-starch diet. The only time Elizabeth has abandoned her weight watching was in pregnancy. Pregnancy endowed her with a sweet tooth, which she appeased with ice cream, cream cake, and cereal sprinkled with glucose.

*

Diana forgoes breakfast and often has no more than a salad for lunch. "I have to watch my waistline," she says. Like Elizabeth, she takes her tea without sugar. But less strong-willed than her mother-in-law, she is sometimes tempted to nibble candy between meals, a failing she shares with Elizabeth's mother (though the queen mother prefers chocolates).

*

Most stringent dieter of the lot is Anne's husband, Mark, who never touches bread, butter, potatoes, or sugar. Instead, he keeps athletically fit mainly on lean meat and green vegetables. He eschews fancy food of all kinds, which is perhaps as well since Anne is no cook; scrambled eggs and fried sausages are about the limit of her culinary ability. Diana, however, is a trained Cordon Bleu cook. While eating little enough herself, she sees to it that Charles is well fed. "She's always trying to fatten me up," he grumbles good-naturedly.

*

Charles is especially partial to smoked salmon and scrambled eggs. Also bread-and-butter pudding, a dish for which he has his own way-out recipe. In addition to the usual ingredients—bread, raisins, and milk—he also stirs in black treacle, chopped bananas, and a spoonful or two of brandy. He devised the recipe himself while taking a naval catering course.

*

When eating in her private dining room, Elizabeth never touches wine, opting for water or orange squash instead.

Even at royal receptions she will often sip orange squash instead of sherry. And while guests at palace banquets are served a different rare wine with each course, she herself will toy with the same single glass of wine throughout.

Philip likes beer with his lunch, white wine with dinner, sometimes whiskey and soda as a nightcap. Son-in-law Mark, despite his stringent dieting, also likes the occasional beer. Anne prefers Coke. So does Andrew. Margaret liked whiskey instead of wine with her dinner, as her father did, but she recently switched to lemon-barley water for health reasons. Elizabeth's mother is fond of champagne cocktails.

Diana likes a little gin with a lot of tonic, but changes to plain water during pregnancy. Charles likes a dry white wine and champagne—Bollinger '75 is his favorite. He didn't get it at a dinner dance in Auckland during the couple's tour of New Zealand. Whatever it was they got instead, it caused Charles to grimace as he sipped it, take Diana's glass from her, and set both glasses firmly aside.

*

None of the family smoke, though cigarettes and cigars are always available for guests. Elizabeth and her children have never smoked. Philip, as a young naval officer, smoked a pipe and the occasional hand-rolled cigarette but gave it up at Elizabeth's request when they married. Philip smoked his last cigarette at a stag party the night before their wedding. Subsequently, he carried a spare button around with him which he would pop into his mouth and suck when the craving for a cigarette came upon him.

Like many another reformed smoker, he is a clean-air addict, ordering windows opened and rooms sprayed with air freshener as soon as dinner guests have departed. "Let's get this smog out of here," he says.

*

Some men crave a cigarette as soon as they awake in the morning. With Philip it is a cup of tea. A maid brings it to the royal bedroom, and he drinks it sitting up in bed. Elizabeth prefers to wait until after breakfast and then brews her own pot of tea. China tea is her favorite, and she is fussy about how it is brewed. When she travels she always takes a canister of her favorite tea along with her, finding it an excellent reviver between public engagments. There was near panic among her staff on one trip to America when the precious tea canister went astray en route to Washington, DC. She was due at the White House at any moment, and her personal servants, who had arrived ahead of her, knew she would be expecting her customary cup of tea. In desperation, her footman ransacked the White House kitchen in search of an alternative. But all he could find were tea bags. They would have to do, it seemed. He made a sample cup. It looked and tasted far from what the queen usually drank. At that moment the presidential butler appeared in the kitchen. The problem was explained to him and quickly resolved. "I'll let you have my own packet of tea," he said. "I like a good strong brew myself."

*

While Elizabeth brews her own pot of tea for breakfast, Philip prefers coffee. Favorite breakfast dishes are boiled eggs (two each), bacon and eggs, sausages, kidneys, and kippers. They finish with two small triangular pieces of toast each, spread with marmalade or honey, and with fruit, an apple or peach or a few grapes.

*

Elizabeth is partial to eggs. But she got rather more than she bargained for on a visit to Sweden. The Swedish royal chef naturally inquired of her aides what she would like for breakfast. "Eggs," they told him. "The queen always likes an egg." It was only later that he realized he had not asked how she liked her eggs done. He remedied his oversight by swamping the breakfast table with eggs done in every conceivable guise—boiled, fried, poached, scrambled, and as omelets.

*

At one time Philip liked to cook his own breakfast and bought himself an electric frying pan. However, their private dining room is located next door to the sitting room which is also Elizabeth's study. The smell of frying not only trickled through, but lingered on, causing official visitors to the royal study to wrinkle their noses. Elizabeth had a quiet word with her husband, and his culinary efforts stopped.

*

The china on the royal family's private dining table is gold-trimmed and embossed with Elizabeth's royal cipher, **EIIR**, surmounted by a small gold crown. Knives, forks, and spoons are antique silver. So are the condiment sets. Even the butter, which comes from the royal dairy at Windsor Castle, is stamped with a crown. But the marmalade and honey they spread on their toast often appears on the breakfast table in the original glass pots.

*

If you think being royal entitles you to eat anything you want at a moment's notice, think again. Menus at Buckingham Palace are always scheduled a day ahead. The royal chef gives Elizabeth a choice of three dishes for each course. She deletes whatever she does not want.

Nor does the food come piping hot. So vast is Buckingham Palace that the royal dining room is nearly a quarter mile from the kitchen and two floors higher up. So food makes the trip in a heated trolley and is then warmed up afresh on hot plates. For royal banquets the food is kept warm in a room fitted with heated compartments adjoining the banquet hall.

*

American presidents and other dignitaries can at least be sure of getting their favorite dishes on future visits to Buckingham Palace or Windsor Castle. The computer used to keep the royal accounts and to ensure that the larder is fully stocked has additionally been programmed not only with the recipes of the royal family's favorite dishes but also with the culinary likes and dislikes of monarchs, presidents, and world statesmen Elizabeth knows she will be hosting from time to time.

*

Since he was obliged to stop cooking his own breakfast because of the smell, Philip's culinary endeavors have been restricted to outdoor barbecues when the family is on vacation at Balmoral Castle in Scotland. For such excursions, he goes along to the kitchen to make his own choice of steak, chicken, sausages, and the like. He does the cooking on a portable barbecue equipped with a revolving spit, resplendent in a chef's apron and hat that Elizabeth bought him for a birthday present.

*

Busy as he is in so many different directions, Philip is seldom home for lunch. "If he takes on much more, he soon won't be here even for breakfast," Elizabeth was heard to sigh once. As it is, she frequently lunches alone. The meal extends to only two courses. Meat and a few vegetables are eaten with a side plate of salad, followed by crackers and cream cheese. The cream cheese, like the butter, is made in the royal dairy at Windsor.

*

Elizabeth is as partial to cream cheese at lunchtime as she is to eggs at breakfast. But there was an occasion in Australia once when she didn't get it. It happened at Perth, where there was an outbreak of poliomyelitis at the time. To avoid any chance of Elizabeth contracting the disease, royal servants took along her own food, drink, china, glass-ware, even table linens and cooking pots. When she landed, the whole lot was loaded into a refrigerated truck that would travel with her. Just as the truck was about to pull away, the sevants realized that the queen's favorite cream cheese had been overlooked. With the truck already secured, it had to be handed to the driver. At lunchtime, Elizabeth, having eaten her main course, looked around for her cream cheese. Again it had been overlooked, and her footman dashed off to get it from the truck driver. "No one told me it was the queen's cheese," mumbled the embarrassed Aussie. "I thought it was my tucker. I ate it."

*

Dinner in Elizabeth and Philip's private dining room at the palace runs to three courses. There is no starter and no sweet course. Favorite dishes include saddle of lamb, lamb cutlets, creamed chicken, filet steak, sole, whiting, and halibut, served with appropriate vegetables and a side plate of salad. Fresh beans and peas are favorite vegetables, though Philip is also partial to spinach. Instead of a sweet, Elizabeth and Philip have a second savory dish, perhaps kidneys and bacon or cheese soufflé or scrambled eggs topped with anchovies. Then comes fruit. Elizabeth usually has an apple, while Philip prefers a few grapes. Coffee concludes the meal. Elizabeth takes hers white and unsweetened. Philip takes his black with a little sugar.

*

These days, pages and footmen no longer hover around the royal family at mealtimes. When dining alone, Elizabeth and Philip much prefer to serve themselves. That way, they can converse freely on family matters without fear of being overheard and some item of conversation perhaps filtering through to the gossip columns. But there is a footman on duty just outside the closed door of the dining room, and a bell push on the dining table enables them to buzz if they want anything. In other ways, too, royal meals have become considerably less formal in recent years. Unless they have guests, Elizabeth and Philip no longer bother to don evening dress for dinner.

*

But royal informality can go only so far, as Princess Margaret revealed when invited to a supper party that proved to be slightly too informal, at least by royal standards. Initially, Margaret was thrilled to find that she was expected to sit on the floor and hold her plate in her hand. Then she spilled her supper on the floor. "I can't seem to manage without a table," she said. "We always have one at home—even for picnics." Her host obligingly found a folding card table for her to sit at.

*

Just down the road from Buckingham Palace, at Clarence House, Elizabeth's mother continues to adhere to the old traditions, changing into a long evening dress for dinner even if she has only the television set for company. She often eats dinner while watching television. Now in her eighties, she also likes the luxury of breakfast in bed while going through the day's mail. Plump though she is, she does not bother with weight watching and never has. Invariably there is an open box of chocolates close to hand on which she nibbles between meals. Unlike her daughter's modest three-course meal at the palace, her own dinner often extends to five courses—soup, fish, meat, sweet, and cheese—and for a sweet she enjoys nothing so much as a steamed pudding.

*

Of course, things are very different at Buckingham Palace if Elizabeth and Philip are entertaining guests. Then there is an abundance of servants in attendance. Even the smallest and most informal royal dinner parties requires not less than:

- three chefs
- two maids (to make toast and coffee)
- two pages (to serve the food)
- the royal steward (to supervise and do the carving)
- a butler (for the wine)
- two underbutlers (to lay the dining table)
- a footman (to fetch and carry for the pages)
- two washers-up

*

For small dinner parties Elizabeth usually wears a short evening dress and Philip a tuxedo. They sit, not at each end of the mahogany dining table, but midway along, facing each other, the better to join in the conversation. Between them, centered on the table, is a silver statuette of Elizabeth on horseback. The meal usually starts with either consommé or a fish dish. The main dish is usually either lamb, roast chicken, or filet steak, served with vegetables and salad. The salad comes on kidney-shaped glass plates that fit snugly beside the dinner plates. Sherry is served with consommé, white wine with fish, a choice of red or white with the meat or chicken, and another, sweeter, white wine with the sweet. But Elizabeth will have only a single glass of wine before switching to orange squash or water. Fresh fruit salad is a favorite sweet dish at royal dinner parties. After the sweet comes the fruit and port. For fruit there is a choice of grapes, peaches, apples, oranges, or bananas, plus cherries and strawberries when they are in season. The decanter of port circulates in accordance with time-honored tradition. It is set on the table in front of Elizabeth (though she never touches it) and circulates from her always in a clockwise direction. One circuit of the table complete, the butler collects it and conveys it around the table to place it in front of Philip. He may or may not top up his glass before passing the decanter clockwise again, never counter-clockwise. So if a guest to Philip's right downs his port rather quickly, he must wait patiently until the decanter has made another circuit before he can indulge in a refill. Fruit and port are followed by coffee and brandy. Although neither Elizabeth nor Philip smokes, there are always cigars and a choice of cigarettes, Virginian or Turkish, for their guests. For small private dinner parties at the palace, Elizabeth no longer observes the ritual of having her lady guests withdraw at the end of the meal so that the men can enjoy a spot of man talk. But for the dinner parties at Windsor Castle, Balmoral Castle, or Sandringham, where there are sometimes as many as forty guests for dinner, the tradition is still observed. However, if the man talks seems to her to be going on for too long, Elizabeth will send a page to remind Philip that it is time to rejoin the ladies.

*

If you think Elizabeth's private dinner parties a shade elaborate, you should see a royal banquet at Buckingham Palace or Windsor Castle (where Elizabeth hosted President and Mrs. Reagan). Preparations for that start weeks ahead, when the royal gold is brought out of storage, all five tons of it, and specially burnished. A royal banquet involves not only Elizabeth's entire domestic staff— steward, housekeeper, chefs, pages, footmen, maids, butlers, underbutlers, porters, and washers-up—but up to 150 additional staff hired through a London domestic agency. Specially trained "table deckers" lay out the state dining table (which has up to nineteen extensions), using measuring sticks to ensure that every place setting, every goblet, every condiment set is meticulously aligned. The

63

century-old damask tablecloths that cover the table and its many extensions are so big and so heavy that they have to be wheeled into position on trolleys before being unrolled. Some of the gold table pieces are even heavier, so massive that it takes four strong men to lift them into place. On the day of the banquet, royal pages and footmen don their resplendent state liveries, black and gold for the pages, scarlet and gold for footmen. The corners of the banquet hall are piled high with flowers—roses, lilies, orchids—and grapes. Into all this splendor Elizabeth makes an appropriately ceremonial entry, with two of her top aides *walking backward* before her. She shimmers with jewels. The table itself glints with gold and crystal. Even the dinner plates are gold. "At least they don't break if you drop them," is Philip's customary quip. To prevent the gold being scratched, plates and smaller items are conveyed to and from the banquet hall in large leather buckets, with a servant titled the Yeoman of the Gold carefully counting each item and checking it for possible scratching afterward.

*

The only time pudding appears on Elizabeth's private dining table is at Christmas. The menu for the royal Christmas dinner at Windsor Castle never varies. Here it is:

Lobster Cocktail

Roast Turkey

Sage and Onion Stuffing

Sausages

Glazed Carrots   Roast Potatoes   Brussel Sprouts

Bread Sauce   Cranberry Jelly

Christmas Pudding

White Sauce   Brandy Butter

Hot Mince Pies

With usually more than thirty members of the family gathered around the dining table, it takes two large, plump turkeys to feed them all. The turkeys are specially reared and fattened on Elizabeth's private estate at Sandringham. The vegetables are grown in the royal kitchen garden at Windsor.

The royal steward carves the turkeys. Liveried footmen take around the vegetables. Rare wines are drunk from crystal goblets, and the Christmas pudding, brandy flames dancing over it, is ceremonially carried in by the royal chef.

Love and Marraige

Nothing has caused the royal family so much soul-searching—and occasional heartbreak—over the years than the question of love and marriage. Elizabeth's uncle, King Edward VIII, later Duke of Windsor, had to sacrifice his crown in order to marry the woman he loved, Wallis Simpson, a twice-divorced American. Elizabeth's sister, Margaret, took the other course and sacrificed the man she loved, Peter Townsend, a World War II fighter ace, in order to retain her royal position. Elizabeth's cousin Prince Michael of Kent was forced to renounce his place in the line of succession to the throne in order to marry the Baroness Marie-Christine von Reibnitz, a Catholic whose previous marriage had been annulled. And Andrew would assuredly have found himself confronted with the same hard choice had he not distanced himself from actress Koo Stark before their love affair reached a more serious level.

*

Two ancient laws, one dating back a little over two hundred years and the other even further, dictate whom members of the royal family may or may not marry. The one that hindered Prince Michael is the oldest. It first saw the light of day in 1701 and states that Britain's crown cannot pass to a Catholic or anyone who marries a

Catholic. "A terrible slight on Catholics," the Catholic Archbishop of Glasgow terms it, and in recent years there have been political efforts to rescind it, but nothing has so far come of them. So Michael, in order to wed a Catholic, had formally to renounce any claim to the throne, though the fact may not have worried him too much. With fifteen others of the family ahead of him in line at the time, his chance of ever becoming king seemed pretty remote.

*

Even Philip found himself with a slight problem of religion before his marriage to Elizabeth. He was not a Catholic, but neither was he a member of the Church of England, having been baptized into the Greek Orthodox Church. The problem was resolved by a second, private baptism, this time into the Church of England. "It isn't everyone who gets married within a couple of months of being baptized," quipped Philip.

*

The second law that hinders freedom of choice in the matter of marriage dates from 1772 and lays down that no member of the royal family may marry without the consent of the reigning sovereign. Penalties for breaking the law are harsh. A royal who marries without the sovereign's consent can be deprived of land, goods, and civil rights. For legal purposes, the marriage itself becomes null and void, and children born to the couple are classed as illegitimate. It was all dreamed up by George III when two of his brothers entered into what he regarded as "scandalous" marriages. One married a widow, the other a girl born illegitimate. Elizabeth may wish it were not part of British law, but it is, and a part that is her personal responsibility. The result has been considerable soul-searching on her part. In Michael's case, she gave her consent provided he renounced any claim to the crown (which he did). In Margaret's case, her consent was not forthcoming. There was no problem over consent when Charles asked to marry Diana. She was not a Catholic and she hadn't a blot on her virginal escutcheon, unlike one or two others with whom Charles may have previously fancied himself in love. Andrew never reached the point of seeking consent to marry Koo Stark, but there can have been no doubt that, given her history of a porn movie and love affairs, consent would not have been forthcoming.

*

In a sense, Margaret was unlucky. Elizabeth was new to the throne in those days and more dependent on those who advised her. And they were men of the old school—Tommy Lascelles, the private secretary she inherited from her father; Winston Churchill, the prime minister she also inherited; and Anthony Eden, who succeeded Churchill as Britain's prime minister. All took the same hard line: The queen's sister could not conceivably marry a man who had been married before. Townsend had divorced his first wife. Yet a few years later, when Margaret married Tony Armstrong-Jones, the royal guest list was sprinkled with his divorced relatives. There was the bridegroom's mother, divorced and remarried; his stepmother, also divorced; and his father, twice divorced and accompanied in Westminster Abbey on the wedding day by the young stewardess who was his third wife. As for Margaret and Tony, well, they too are now divorced.

But Margaret and Peter Townsend were also to blame. Elizabeth, longing for her sister's happiness, sought desperately for a way out of the dilemma, and found one. She could give consent, she realized, if Margaret would renounce any claim to the crown (as their cousin Michael did later). With Elizabeth already the mother of two children at the time, Charles and Anne, there was little likelihood of Margaret ever succeeding her. But renouncing her place in the line of succession would also have meant giving up her annual state allowance as a royal princess. She talked things over with Peter Townsend, and together they decided that it would be impossible for love to survive on his air-force pay. So she renounced him instead in a heartrending statement that he helped her to write.

*

Despite her public renunciation of Peter Townsend, Margaret continued to see him from time to time in secret, continued to seek a way out that would enable her both to marry him and still be paid her royal allowance. In the end, it was Townsend who got tired of waiting. Margaret read of his engagement to another girl in a newspaper. Piqued, she crumpled the newspaper into a ball and hurled it across the room. On the rebound from Peter, she married Tony.

*

A later British prime minister, the pragmatic Harold Wilson, could almost certainly have devised a way out for Margaret that would have let Elizabeth off the hook, as he did when Elizabeth's cousin, George, Earl of Harewood, sought permission to marry his former secretary. He had already had a child by her and been divorced by his wife in consequence. Elizabeth's problem was that as well as being queen she is also Supreme Governor of the Church of England, chief custodian of its social, moral, and religious values. As such, how could she possibly consent to the marriage of a cousin who had behaved in such a fashion? Yet the well-being of the illegitimate child clearly required that mother and father marry. Harold Wilson's solution was to have the matter discussed at a meeting of his cabinet, thus making it, if only technically, a matter of government rather than one of religion. It was with relief that Elizabeth received and acted upon his subsequent prime ministerial advice (as she was constitutionally obliged to do) that she should consent to the proposed marriage. The same pragmatic device could be used if Margaret, now divorced from Snowdon, should wish to marry again. "No fear of that," Margaret has assured her sister.

*

Of all recent royal romances, Princess Margaret's wooing by photographer Tony Armstrong-Jones was the best-kept secret. Tony borrowed a hideaway cottage overlooking the Thames for lovers' meetings. Margaret would slip in disguised in a kerchief and dark glasses. She wore a similar disguise for theater outings, occupying seats booked in the name of "Mr. and Mrs. Gordon." The "Mrs. Gordon" who made the bookings was in fact her maid, Ruby Gordon. She would get other already well-publicized boyfriends to escort her to parties with Tony, who was there ostensibly to take photographs for the glossy magazines and who arrived separately on his motorcycle. Margaret's mother aided the romantic conspiracy (as she was to aid Charles and Diana later) by "commissioning" Tony to take endless photographs of her London home and her weekend retreat at Windsor. Tony played his part by always arriving with a vast quantity of photographic equipment. So successful was the conspiracy that even royal servants— with the exception of Margaret's maid, Ruby—were surprised when the couple's betrothal was eventually announced.

*

Time was when royalty married only royalty. So effectively did Queen Victoria arrange the marriages of her children that she lived to see her grandchildren become Emperor of Germany, Empress of Russia, and queens of no fewer than five countries—Sweden, Norway, Spain, Greece, and Rumania. Times have changed, and royal marriages are no longer arranged (even if romances with "unacceptable" men and women are firmly discouraged). True, the naval lieutenant the future Elizabeth II married had been born a Greek prince. But her sister Margaret married a working photographer, her daughter married a junior army officer, and her eldest son married a kindergarten teacher (even if Diana was also the daughter of an earl). One of her cousins married a Danish-born secretary, another the daughter of a country landowner, and yet another, Princess Alexandra, wed a company director.

*

Queen Victoria was the last of the great royal matchmakers. Over the course of two generations she would brook no obstacle when it came to spinning her web of royal marriages. She married her eldest son, Britain's next king, to a Danish princess. Years later, for his eldest son, a future king himself, her choice fell upon a German princess, Mary of Teck. Marriage was only seven weeks away when he died from pneumonia. Now it was his younger brother, George, who would be king—and Victoria still saw Mary of Teck as Britain's future queen. Eighteen months later, thanks to his grandmother's assiduous scheming, George and Mary were married and in due course became king and queen, as Victoria had planned. "I am very fond of you, but not very much in love with you," George told Mary almost on their wedding night. Nevertheless, they had six children, and he remained a faithful husband and she a loyal wife. "My dearest husband, King George V," she wrote, recording his death after more than forty years of marriage.

*

The last of the royal family's arranged marriages was that of Elizabeth's Aunt Mary, the Princess Royal. As a young woman in the 1920s she was married off to a friend of her father, "Lucky" Lascelles, heir to the Harewood earldom. If the fifteen-year difference in their ages was not necessarily an obstacle to married happiness (Charles is nearly that much older than Diana), the difference in their temperaments certainly was. Mary was a shy and sensitive girl, "Lucky" a coarse, hard-living character, very much a man's man. Mary's eldest brother, the Prince of Wales (later Duke of Windsor), was against the marriage, realizing how different in character they were, but their father, King George V, was not the type to tolerate opposition to anything on which he had set his mind. Once married, Mary found herself hauled off to the Harewood mansion in the wilds of northern England, where she lived a lonely married life while her husband dashed around pursuing the hunting, shooting, and racing existence to which he was addicted.

*

Margaret was sixteen when she first fell in love with Peter Townsend. Elizabeth was even younger, a child of thirteen, when she fell in love with Philip. He was nineteen at the time, a tall, blond, arrogantly handsome naval cadet. They met when Elizabeth's father took her with him on a visit to the Royal Naval College at Dartmouth, where Philip was training. For the rest of the day she followed Philip around like a pet lamb and blushed scarlet each time he spoke to her. "She was in love from the beginning," according to Philip's uncle, the late Earl Mountbatten, who was there at the time. "He's so terribly good-looking," Elizabeth confided to her governess. Margaret, eight at the time, was more impressed by his voracious appetite and the tremendous quantity of shrimp he ate when the three of them had tea together.

*

Because of the war, with Philip away at sea, theirs was largely a correspondence courtship. They met only at infrequent intervals, when Philip was in Britain on leave. If Elizabeth was a one-man girl from the outset, Philip was not always a one-girl man. He dated other girls wherever his ship docked, in South Africa and Australia as well as Britain. But with the possibility of one day marrying Elizabeth at the back of his mind, he never permitted himself to become seriously involved, never even dated the same girl twice. One who telephoned his grandmother's home when he was on leave in London in the hope of a second date was curtly informed that he had "gone away." He had—but only to his uncle's home a few streets away. Another who telephoned was similarly told, "Prince Philip has rejoined his ship." It was only later that it dawned on her that the voice that had given her that piece of information had sounded suspiciously like Philip's own.

*

Among the first to know that Elizabeth and Philip had reached the courtship stage were a couple named Fallon with whom Philip became friendly when his ship docked in Australia toward the end of the war. "You've picked the wrong one," Judy Fallon joked, showing him a newspaper picture of Elizabeth and Margaret. "Margaret's the better looking." Philip snapped back, "You wouldn't say that if you knew them. Elizabeth is sweet and kind, just like her mother."

*

Philip has always been very fond of his royal mother-in-law. And she enjoys his salty jokes. As a young naval officer, he had little money when he first knew her, and the first Christmas present he bought her was a book of poems picked up secondhand from a street market.

Invited to join the royal family on holiday at Balmoral in courtship days, Philip arrived there without pajamas (he never wore them), without slippers (you didn't need them aboard ship), and without tweeds (he couldn't afford them). But he did have a tuxedo borrowed from his uncle, Earl Mountbatten and a gun, also borrowed. Instead of tweeds, he went shooting with Elizabeth's father, King George VI, in flannel trousers and a woolly sweater plus naval walking-out shoes. The heathery grouse moors soon ruined the shoes, and he had to spend a day indoors while the shoes were mended for him.

One day when he and the king were out shooting together, Philip decided upon a last-minute change of position. He moved just as the king opened fire—and got well peppered with shot.

*

Philip was always slightly in awe of Elizabeth's father. But the king liked him well enough. "Philip's the right man for Lilibet," he confided in a friend. "But I don't think he realizes what he's letting himself in for. One day Lilibet will be queen and he will be consort. And that's the hardest job in the world."

*

On his meager naval pay Philip could hardly afford the sort of engagement ring fit for a princess (the ring Charles bought for Diana a generation later cost $42,000). His mother helped out by giving him a ring his father had given her. He took it a jeweler to have the stones reset. Unfortunately, he could only guess at the size of Elizabeth's finger. It was not until he gave it to her that he discovered that the ring was too big. Hence the ease with which she can still spin it round and round on her finger.

*

Philip's naval buddies threw a stag party the night before the wedding. The result was that he woke up on his wedding morning with something of a hangover and was furious when his Mountbatten cousin, David, who was also his best man, leaked the story to the newspapers—so furious that it was several years before he would again speak to the offender.

*

On Elizabeth's end, almost everything went wrong on her wedding day. Her tiara cracked as she was putting it on her head and had to be whipped away for repairs. She wanted to wear the pearls her parents had given her as a wedding gift but found they were on display with the other wedding presents. Her secretary went to fetch them from nearby Kensington Palace. He duly arrived back with the pearls—plus an escort of three policemen sent along to make quite sure that he was who he said he was. To top it all, just as Elizabeth was about to leave for Westminster Abbey, her bridal bouquet was nowhere to be found. For a few minutes there was near panic, with everyone rushing and searching everywhere. Calm was restored only with the return of a footman who had been along to reserve himself a window place from which to watch the bride's departure. "Try the refrigerator," he said. "I put the flowers in there to keep them fresh."

*

The flowers, in fact, were less a bouquet than a simple spray of white orchids. They were one of the few things Philip, as bridegroom, paid for on their wedding day. A more romantic man than his public image might suggest, these days he positively showers Elizabeth with flowers on their wedding anniversary each year—carnations, roses, camellias and lilies-of-the-valley, all white.

*

Marriage, in 1947, marked the end of a long period of courtship. They had known each other for more than eight years and had been courting seriously for about four. Their wedding anniversary falls on November 20.

*

Ruggedly handsome as he was—indeed, still is—Philip continued to attract the opposite sex even after marriage. The first time he and Elizabeth visited Australia together, tour organizers were puzzled why there were always so many more girls on one side of the royal route than the other. Then the answer dawned on them: That was the side on which Philip always sat. Wherever he went, feminine reaction was blatant. In Sydney girls pursued him with wolf whistles. In Hobart they blew kisses. And one girl who was presented to him gave him a wink of such come-hither content that even the normally unflappable Philip was seen to blush.

Charles, from his teens on, was to be similarly tempted by girls wherever he went. In the less awestruck atmosphere of his young manhood, it was to be kisses, kisses, all the way. As a bachelor prince, he rather enjoyed it. What he did not enjoy was the way his official hosts in various parts of the world tried to pair him off with their daughters or nieces. The suspicion that President Nixon was hoping to see daughter Tricia end up as Princess of Wales did much to spoil his 1970 visit to the United States.

Marriage to Diana has not stopped the kissing. Wherever Charles goes, even with Diana right beside him, girls continue to kiss him or ask him to kiss them. These days, with Diana watching, he finds that embarrassing, too.

*

Fortunately, Diana was not around the morning he went swimming in Australia and found two topless girls pursuing him into the water. Fortunately, too, his entourage managed to head the girls off before they came close enough to Charles to press themselves against him.

Andrew, on the other hand, being still a bachelor, felt no embarrassment over romping in the surf with two topless lovelies when his ship docked in Barbados in 1983; he even stripped off his own shorts and waved them at onlookers. With Charles married, Andrew is now the world's number-one eligible bachelor. Even before Charles was married, Andrew, a ruggedly handsome six-footer with a toothy grin, was already provoking a bigger reaction among the girls. Visiting Canada with his parents for the 1976 Olympics at the age of sixteen, he was pursued by squealing teenagers wherever he went. Those who couldn't get to him personally—and few did—thrust love notes, love poems, telephone numbers, and party invitations into the hands of royal aides. When he was a naval cadet and his ship made a courtesy call at Pensacola, Florida, the switchboard burned red-hot with calls from girls eager to show him the sights. Andrew, on that occasion, had other sights in mind—the topless waitresses in Trader Jon's Bar Pigalle.

*

Princesses hitherto have escaped such adulation from the opposite sex. But Diana's arrival on the royal scene has changed that. To her considerable embarrassment, young men sometimes kiss her during the course of royal walkabouts as enthusiastically as girls kiss Charles. "You're supposed to shake hands," she reprimanded one young man primly. Older men, if less demonstrative, are equally captivated by her. Pierre Trudeau, initially rather cool toward the couple's 1983 royal tour of Canada, had a change of heart as soon as he met Diana; he began inviting himself to almost every function she and Charles attended. "Ask me about her beautiful blue eyes," he cooed at reporters, while Brian Peckford, premier of Newfoundland, sighed jestingly, "I guess I've just fallen in love."

*

Walkabout kisses and jesting endearments may be permissible, if sometime embarrassing to Diana, but anything more could be highly dangerous. Under ancient British law, it is treason, punishable by death, to "violate" the wife of the monarch's eldest son. The same goes for the monarch herself or the monarch's wife if there is a king on the throne. Historically, of course, kings and princes have always been free to violate other men's wives.

*

With arranged marriages now a thing of the past, chance encounters can result in royal weddings. Margaret and her ex-husband, Snowdon, in fact met at a wedding. But while she was a guest, he was there merely to take the wedding photographs. Elizabeth's cousin Richard, Duke of Gloucester, met his future wife at a tea party when he was a student at Cambridge and she was over from Denmark attending a language school there. Another royal cousin, Edward, Duke of Kent, met his duchess when, along with fellow officers from the Royal Scots Greys, he was invited to a garden party at her parents' home and she partnered him at tennis. Anne met Mark on the royal equivalent of a blind date. Anne was seventeen at the time, not long out of boarding school. She was invited to a dinner party held in connection with some horse trials in which she was taking part. Mark, then a young cadet at the Royal Military College, was also invited along—simply to make an even number at the dinner table. Charles first met Diana when he was going around with her sister Sarah. Sarah invited him home, and he was out shooting there, plodding across a freshly plowed field, when he ran into Diana, at that time a leggy sixteen-year-old home on holiday from school.

*

If Charles, on the occasion of that first meeting, gave Diana no more than a passing glance and a casual greeting,

79

the effect on her was different. From then on she was always "a little in love" with Charles and, as though saving herself for him, never had any other serious boyfriend. Charles, by contrast, had a load of girlfriends, falling in and out of love with almost clockwork regularity.

*

Curiously, Charles was a late starter where girls were concerned, shy and uncomfortable in their presence. "A sweet virgin boy," one girl labeled him when he was at university. Then Lucia Santa Cruz, daughter of the Chilean ambassador to London, came into his life. She was in Cambridge, research assistant to Lord Butler, at the time Charles was studying there. Lord Butler has denied the story that he allowed them the use of his private rooms so that they could be alone together, but certainly from that time on Charles' love life really took off. From then on, it was girls, girls, girls all the way. If most were no more than ships passing in the night, there were some others he came close to marrying.

He had a long and romantic relationship with the Duke of Wellington's daughter, Jane. On his side, at least, things became so serious at one point that he had his grandmother give Jane pointers as to what life would be like as Princess of Wales. But Jane shied away from marriage.

After Jane there was Davina Sheffield, tall and leggy, cousin of Lord McGowan. They went away secretly on holiday together, and Charles at the time was clearly in love with her. But any hope he had of marrying her and making her Princess of Wales foundered abruptly when gossip concerning her earlier love life appeared in the newspapers. As British law will not permit a Catholic queen, the British people would not accept one whose premarital life permitted more than one interpretation.

*

A highly charged relationship with millionaire's daughter Anna Wallace came close to seeing her, not Diana, become Princess of Wales. For more than half a year Charles was almost head over heels in love with her. Over that period, she was constantly at the palace, closeted with Charles in his private apartment, and royal servants who glimpsed her as she came and went were more and more convinced that they were seeing their future queen. She was his personal guest at his grandmother's eightieth birthday ball—and it was there that things went wrong.

Charles, that night, with family around him, was more concerned with playing the prince than acting the lover. Anna took offense to a degree that saw her upbraiding him loudly enough for others to hear.

"I've never been treated so badly in my life," she lambasted him. "Nobody—not even you—behaves that way to me." And, like Cinderella, away from the ball she fled.

It was only after his quarrel with Anna that he began paying serious attention to Diana. Previously, when she had been invited to stay with the royals at Balmoral or Sandringham, it was because they saw her as a possible future bride for Andrew, not Charles. But now Charles began wooing her. It was as his guest that she stayed aboard the royal yacht for the annual yachting week at Cowes that summer. The rest is history.

*

If Charles was a late starter where girls were concerned, Andrew was an early one, pursuing them so enthusiastically during coed schooldays at Gordonstoun that he earned the nickname "Randy Andy." Spells of shore leave after he went into the navy were enlivened, in turn, by a beauty queen, a ballet dancer, and a brace of models. But these were romantic dalliances, not love

81

affairs. His relationship with Koo Stark (born Kathleen Norris), an American actress whose main claim to fame was a porn movie entitled *Emily*, was very different. She swept him off his feet from the moment he first met her in a London disco. Shortly after, a British task force sailed south to recapture the Falklands, and Andy, as a naval helicopter pilot, went with it. Deprived of any form of female companionship during that brief but bloody campaign and during the long months that followed when his ship remained on duty in the South Atlantic long after most of the victorious task force had returned, Andrew poured out his feelings for Koo in letter and on tape. Returning to Britain finally after an absence of nearly six months, he flew straight into her arms. Given a spell of extended leave, he was constantly in her company, sometimes at her flat, sometimes in his private apartment at the palace. He gave her his naval dog tags as a symbol of his love, and she wore them around her neck.

Unworldly as they are in so many ways, his parents knew nothing of Koo's past, and when Andrew asked to invite her to Balmoral, they obliged. Equally, he prevailed upon his Aunt Margaret to lend him her villa on the island of Mustique, where he took Koo for a romantic vacation. But by then Elizabeth and Philip had learned (from the newspapers) of Koo's movie background and previous love affairs. Telephone calls to Mustique from Buckingham Palace resulted in Andrew cutting short his holiday and flying home while Koo went to her mother's home in Miami. And that was that.

*

Diana's main virtue, in the eyes of both the royal family and the British public, was that she was a girl without a "past, a virgin with no record of previous love affairs." Elizabeth and Philip already visualized her as a possible future daughter-in-law—though as a possible bride for Andrew rather than Charles—when they first invited her to stay at Balmoral in 1979. She had just turned eighteen at the time. But it was Charles, not Andrew, who a year later was to start thinking of her in terms of marriage. His grandmother was among the first to spot which way the wind of romance was blowing. A close friend of Diana's grandmother, with whom she once played piano duets and who is today her lady-in-waiting, she has known Diana since she was a baby. Delighted by the possibility that her grandson might marry her best friend's granddaughter, the queen mother decided to give love a helping hand. In the late summer of 1980, when the rest of the royals had all left Balmoral, she invited Diana to stay with her at Birkhall, her private home on the Balmoral estate. She invited Charles at the same time and afforded the two opportunities to be alone together.

*

That Elizabeth's mother should have taken it upon herself to give young love a helping hand was very much in character. Lacking a similar helping hand herself, she came perilously close to not marrying Elizabeth's father, though not for any lack of wooing on his part. Twice he proposed to her, and twice she turned him down. To marry him and become part of the royal family, she told him, would mean "never again being free to think, speak, or act as I feel I should think, speak, and act." But Elizabeth's father was nothing if not persistent. He proposed a third time, and this time she said yes. "I'm not sure it didn't come as even more of a surprise to me than it did to him," she said afterward.

He was the love of her life, and she was heartbroken when he died at the early age of fifty-six. To keep his memory fresh, she instructed servants at Royal Lodge, their weekend retreat, that his desk there was to be left exactly as it was in his lifetime, set out with his leather blotter and silver inkstand, silver traveling clock, and his favorite photographs—Elizabeth and Margaret as children and one of his wife in those 1920s days when they were first married. It is still like that today.

So great was her grief when he died that her first thought was to withdraw into seclusion and undertake no more royal engagements. She bought herself a ruined castle in the far north of Scotland and withdrew there. It was Winston Churchill who lured her out again. He told her: "The country needs you, Ma'am. Your daughter, the queen, needs you."

*

As heir to the throne, Charles, despite the fact that he was thirty-two at the time, still needed his mother's formal permission to marry Diana. He was so sure of getting it that he proposed to Diana first and sought formal consent later. Like a dutiful son-in-law-to-be, he also asked Diana's father for permission to marry his daughter. "I don't know what he would have said if I'd turned him down," joked Earl Spencer.

For Charles, there was a highly embarrassing moment immediately following his betrothal to Diana. He was in Scotland, attending an official luncheon. Peter Balfour, chairman of the Scottish Council, decided to propose a toast to the prince and his bride-to-be. Unfortunately, he got the name wrong. Instead of proposing a toast to Charles and Diana, he proposed one to "Prince Charles and Lady *Jane*." Jane is the name of one of Diana's two sisters. It is also the name of the Duke of Wellington's daughter who was once the girl everyone thought Charles would marry.

Charles blushed scarlet as the wrong name came out. "I feel bloody awful, a perfect fool," the unfortunate Balfour apologized hastily.

*

In Queen Victoria's day royal weddings were always solemnized in the privacy of one of the royal chapels at Buckingham Palace or Windsor Castle. More recently, Westminster Abbey has been the traditional venue. Elizabeth's mother, Elizabeth herself, Margaret, and Anne were all married there, and the abbey authorities were mildly disconcerted when Charles and Diana settled on St. Paul's Cathedral. They picked it for its better acoustics, important for a wedding that featured three orchestras, two choirs, and an aria sung by a world-famous soprano, Kiri Te Kanawa.

*

As the wedding approached, Charles and Diana had a private session with the Archbishop of Canterbury, who was to conduct the ceremony. He gave them a lecture on sex and parenthood. Sex, he told them, "is a good thing, given by God, which nevertheless, like all God's gifts, needs to be directed aright."

*

Charles has his own views on marriage. "It's more than just a romantic idea of falling madly in love with someone and having a love affair for the rest of your life," he says. "It's a very strong friendship, shared interests, and ideas in common, plus a great deal of affection. Essentially you must be good friends, and love, I'm sure, grows out of that. To me, marriage—which may be for fifty years—seems to be one of the biggest and most responsible steps taken in one's life. Marriage is not only for the two people who form the marriage. It is also for the children."

*

With most ordinary weddings, it is the bride's mother who plans everything and the bride's father who does most of the paying. Not so when the bridegroom is the next king.

85

When Charles married Diana, his mother and her aides took complete control. Of the 2,300 wedding invitations that went out, the bride's family were allotted a meager two hundred, which made things "a bit difficult," Diana said. But at least her father did not have to pick up the tab. "Thank God for that," said Earl Spencer when he heard that the total cost was around a quarter of a million dollars. In fact, Diana did not even have to pay for her wedding dress. David and Elizabeth Emmanuel, who designed it, gave it to her as a wedding present. The publicity they got in return more than repaid them. The cost of the wedding was partly met by Charles and his mother, who between them shelled out $72,000, and partly by Britain's taxpayers. However, the taxpayers' share was recouped from the sale of television rights, enabling the wedding spectacular to be seen by an estimated 750 million people in fifty-five countries.

*

However, Diana did get her way on some things when it came to arranging the wedding. A modern and determined young woman, she was willing enough to promise to love, honor, comfort, and keep Charles, but not to obey him. So the word *obey* was omitted from her wedding vows. And she wanted only her divorced parents, not her stepmother, sitting in the family pew. She got her way over that, too. Philip, when he married Elizabeth a generation before, was less fortunate. His three sisters, because they were married to Germans—and Germany was Britain's wartime enemy—were not invited to the wedding.

*

Elizabeth lent her son and daughter-in-law her royal yacht for their honeymoon. There was one big drawback, Charles discovered. The yacht's royal cabins have only single beds. Anne and Mark, who also honeymooned on the yacht, overcame the problem by lashing two single beds together. Charles went one better. He had a double bed shipped aboard specially for the honeymoon.

In some ways, it was an extraordinary honeymoon. Apart from the bride, there was only one other woman aboard the yacht, Diana's maid. Everyone else was male—Charles, twelve royal aides, twenty-two ship's officers, two hundred fifty crewmen, and a band of twenty-six musicians.

*

Of all royal love stories, the one that caused the biggest turmoil was that of Elizabeth's uncle, King Edward VIII, and Mrs. Simpson (born Bessie Warfield at Blue Ridge Summit, Pennsylvania). When Mrs. Simpson first came on the scene, the Prince of Wales, as he then was, was already involved in two long-lasting love affairs. One was with American-born Thelma Vanderbilt, who had married into Britain's aristocracy to become Lady Furness, the other with Freda Dudley Ward, a married woman with two children. Ironically, it was Thelma who introduced Mrs. Simpson to the prince and who later, when leaving Britain to visit her twin sister, Gloria Vanderbilt, in New York, asked her to "look after the little man for me and see he doesn't get into any mischief."

Returning to Britain from her New York trip, Thelma quickly realized that Mrs. Simpson had been looking after the prince only too well. Both were guests at his country home, Fort Belvedere, that weekend. "Are you keen on Wallis?" Thelma asked him when he came to her room that night. "Don't be silly," he retorted. But she knew him too well. The following morning she packed her bags again and walked out of his life.

His other love, Freda, found herself summarily dismissed. Time and again she telephoned, to be told that he was not available. Even the royal telephone operator took pity on her and told her eventually, "I'm sorry, Mrs. Ward, but I have instructions not to put you through."

As king, besotted with Mrs. Simpson, Elizabeth's uncle neglected the duties of kingship to jaunt around Europe with her, and he decked her out in the jeweled heirlooms of the royal family. He helped to arrange her divorce (her second) from Ernest Simpson, planning to marry her and make her queen. As king he could give himself permission to marry whom he liked, he thought. But he had reckoned without his mother, his brothers, his sisters-in-law, and Stanley Baldwin, Britain's pipe-smoking, uncompromising prime minister. There was nothing pragmatic about Baldwin. He was not going to bend any rules. In fact, he was busy making his own fresh set of rules: Either give up this idea of marrying a woman already twice divorced or get off the throne, he told Elizabeth's uncle (though he expressed it more diplomatically, of course).

*

It is now part of British history that King Edward VIII sacrificed his throne for love of Mrs. Simpson. The family split that followed was to affect three generations. The ex-king's mother, Queen Mary, a royal of the old school, stolidly refused to have anything to do with a divorced woman and died seventeen years later without ever meeting her American daughter-in-law. She expressed her feelings in a letter to her eldest son soon after he abdicated:

"I do not think you have ever realised the shock which the attitude you took up caused your whole family. My feelings for you as your Mother remain the same, and our being parted, and the cause of it, grieve me beyond words. After all, all my life I have put my Country before everything else, and I simply cannot change now."

If Queen Mary resented Mrs. Simpson because of the abdication, her other daughters-in-law disliked the new one for more personal reasons, classing her as shallow, brittle, and bossy. None of the family went to the wedding, though they were invited. Elizabeth's mother was particularly bitter toward both her brother-in-law and his new wife. The abdication had forced her husband to become king, and she knew his health was not up to it. In her fifteen years as queen she never met either of the Windsors (as the couple now were). On occasions when her once-favorite brother-in-law journeyed from France to Britain to see the brother who was now king, she would pointedly leave the palace before he arrived and stay away until he had gone again. They met again for the first time at her husband's funeral. She hardly spoke to him.

*

Elizabeth's father was less bitter than most toward the elder brother he had always looked up to. He gave him an allowance of $72,000 a year, made him Duke of Windsor, and gave him the additional title of His Royal Highness. But swayed by both family and public feeling, he declined to make Mrs. Simpson, now Duchess of Windsor, similarly a Royal Highness (equivalent to Princess). His brother was furious and promptly—and unofficially—bestowed the title on her himself. A new servant at the couple's home in France aroused Windsor's fury by addressing the duchess as "Your Grace," though he was perfectly correct in doing so.

"It's not 'Your Grace,'" Windsor fumed. "It's Your Royal Highness. You're not in England now, man."

*

Angry and bitter, Windsor refused an invitation to Elizabeth's wedding (because it was addressed to "His Royal Highness the Duke and Her Grace the Duchess of Windsor") and, years later, similarly turned down an invitation to Margaret's wedding. Even the death of Elizabeth's father did nothing to mend the family rift, and it was not until 1970, nearly thirty-four years after the abdication, that the first chink of light showed through what the former Mrs. Simpson has styled "the Asbestos Curtain." It was Charles who began the healing process. Dispatched to France by his mother to represent her at a memorial service for Charles de Gaulle, he also took the opportunity to pay a call on his aging great-uncle. A visit from Elizabeth and Philip followed. Elizabeth later invited them both to London, and this time they accepted, though they did not stay at the palace. When Windsor died and his body was shipped home for entombment in the family vault, Elizabeth invited his widow to the ceremony, sent her own aircraft to fetch her, sat beside her at the memorial service, and took her back to Buckingham Palace to spend the night. For the twice-divorced American who had once hoped to become queen, it was the first time she had been inside the palace for more than thirty-six years.

*

For the royals, married happiness is not helped by all the whispers and rumors that abound about their marriages. France's more spicy magazines make a specialty of seizing on such rumors and turning molehills into mountains. Statistics show that over a period of fourteen years Elizabeth and Philip were on the verge of divorce or separation seventy-three times—according to French magazines. Britain's tabloid newspapers are not yet that bad, though bad enough. Gossip stories about Anne and Mark's marriage in 1981 found him forced to deny publicly that he was having an affair with TV personality Angela Rippon. In fact, they were working on a book together. Mark was especially concerned at the effect the stories were having on Anne, who has a reputation for being a possessive wife. "There has been no harm done between us," he said. "At the same time, when you read something like that, it sows seeds. It puts a thought there that was not there before."

Jokers Royal

The royals were on vacation at Balmoral, their Disneyesque castle in the Scottish Highlands, when suddenly the security alarm was triggered. In the castle itself, armed bodyguards dashed to the part of the building from which the alarm had sounded. In the grounds, more armed guards and police dogs cordoned off the building. Fifty miles away, in the oil-boom city of Aberdeen, police reinforcements piled into squad cars and tore off at top speed in the direction of Elizabeth's Scottish homestead.

It all ended with an embarrassed royal nanny explaining to security men who converged on William's nursery that it was not some terrorist attempt to kidnap her small charge. Charles and Diana's small son, having reached the toddling stage, had decided to explore his nursery surroundings, had found the "panic button" of the alarm system within reach and, childlike, had pressed it.

There was another security alert not long after at Kensington Palace, the couple's London residence. Again William was the unwitting cause. Toddling about the palace gardens, he had toddled right through a protective infrared beam.

William, of course, was still too young to appreciate the joke on these occasions. But if Charles, Anne, and Andrew are anything to go by, the day will come when he will enjoy a good joke at other people's expense. All three have been inveterate practical jokers in their time. Indeed, Charles still is.

A naval destroyer had been placed at his disposal for an official visit to Scotland. During the course of the voyage an impromptu burlesque show was staged for the benefit of the crew, with Charles joining them in the audience. One act was a spoof magician. "Anyone lend me a watch?" he asked. "Have mine," said Charles, handing it over. "The queen gave me it for my twenty-first birthday."

The watch was placed in a bag, and the "magician" pounded it with a hammer. "Don't worry," he assured the audience. "My magical powers will render it whole again."

Unfortunately, they didn't, and Charles, to the horror of the rest of audience, was left with a handful of bits and pieces.

In fact, the whole thing was a put-up job, with Charles in on the act. The watch his mother had supposedly given him for his twenty-first birthday had actually been bought in a junk shop for 70 cents.

*

For generations the royals have been addicted to practical joking. Elizabeth's great-grandfather, King Edward VII, thought it great fun to pop strange objects into the beds of his houseguests. Unsuspecting guests, climbing into bed after an evening spent dining and wining, might find themselves lying on a sprinkling of dried peas, cuddling down with a dead seagull, or even worse, a live lobster. Soda syphons, newly invented in the days when Edward VII was Prince of Wales, also enlivened royal dinner parties. He and his wife, Alexandra, would squirt people with them. The Duke of Windsor, in his youthful days, once made a tadpole sandwich and inserted it among the tidbits being handed around at a royal tea party.

*

Prince Philip was an inveterate practical joker in more youthful days. As a small boy, staying with royal relatives in Europe, he caused a near panic on one occasion by releasing some pigs and chasing them onto the lawn where his relatives were entertaining guests at an outdoor tea party. Elizabeth suffered a great deal from his jokes in the days when they were newlyweds. Once she helped herself to a bun that let out a loud squeaking sound when she bit into it. On another occasion Philip gave her a can labeled "Mixed Nuts." Opening it, she let out a shriek of horror as an imitation snake sprang out.

In those early days of marriage, with Philip still in the navy, Elizabeth flew more than once to be with him in Malta, where he was based. Philip had just taken up polo at the time, and one morning found him and other naval officers exercising their ponies on a beach where Royal Marines were due to stage a mock landing. Philip and his fellows decided to be the enemy. As the marines came ashore, the horsemen held their polo sticks like lances and, Philip in the lead, charged the astonished landing party, yelling, "We are the Knights of Malta!" Needless to say, it was not a joke appreciated by Philip's superiors, and he was later given an official reprimand.

*

Feeling in need of moral support when he first married into the royal family, Philip signed on his old naval buddy, Michael Parker, an exuberant Australian, as his own royal aide. For years they were almost inseparable, a skylarking duo, with Elizabeth happy to join in on their fun and games. When the U.S. ambassador invited them to a fancy dress ball on one occasion they went along dressed as "the waiter, the porter, and the second-story maid."

*

During their spell in Malta together it was arranged for Elizabeth and Philip to pay a semiofficial visit to Philip's native Greece. Because Philip's own small frigate lacked the necessary accommodation for a royal princess (as Elizabeth was at the time), she sailed on a larger vessel with the exuberant Parker along to look after her. Signals between the two ships afforded ample opportunity for comic relief as they sailed toward Greece. "How is the princess?" Philip signaled one morning. "Full of beans," Parker signaled back. Whereupon Philip signaled: "Is that the best you can give her for breakfast?"

*

Philip and Parker were in particularly rollicking form throughout the round-the-world tour Elizabeth undertook soon after her coronation. Most of the trip was by sea and, outward bound, the pair of them staged a traditional crossing-the-line ceremony as their ship passed the equator. Everyone on board who had not crossed the equator before was lined up on deck to appear before the "court" of King Neptune on sundry mock charges. All were found guilty and handed over to the "barber" and his assistant for punishment. Philip's bodyguard, Frank Kelly, played the part of Neptune while Parker was the barber and Philip, a butcher's apron flapping about him and his nose reddened with greasepaint, was his assistant, daubing the guilty ones with lather (a mixture of flour and whitewash) and smearing them with cochineal (to represent blood) while Parker scraped the mess off with an enormous wooden razor. Punishment ended with each victim being pitched backward into the ship's swimming pool. Elizabeth herself, on this occasion, escaped their attentions, having already crossed the equator once before (on a trip to South Africa with her parents) but enjoyed herself filming the whole hilarious business with her movie camera.

*

There were numerous high jinks, too, when Philip, bored with palace life, set out aboard his wife's royal yacht to explore the Antarctic. Elizabeth was not along on that occasion, though Parker was. On one trip ashore, to visit an isolated survey crew, they found the walls of the survey hut decorated with snips of necktie, souvenirs left behind by previous visitors to the lonely outpost. Philip promptly volunteered to have his own necktie snipped in such a good cause and instructed the rest of his party to do likewise. But Parker was not wearing a necktie. To make good the deficiency, Philip promptly whipped out the tail of the Australian's tartan shirt and held it while a piece was scissored off.

Philip also instituted his own crossing-the-line ceremony on the day the royal yacht crossed the Antarctic Circle. With the temperature below freezing, there could be no question of ducking people in the swimming pool, of course. Instead, Philip devised a new royal order—the Order of the Red Nose—and designed certificates to go along with it which he handed out to his aides and members of the yacht's crew. To go with the "order," he also launched a beard-growing contest with prizes for the longest, bushiest, and most colorful beards. The prizes turned out to be razor blades and after-shave lotion.

*

While Philip himself did not take part in the contest, he did go along with the others by growing a blond beard. Back home in Britain, Elizabeth got to hear of all this in radio-telephone calls from the yacht and decided to play a little joke of her own. She and Philip had arranged to meet each

95

other in Portugal, to which country she was due to pay a state visit. Philip arrived first with the royal yacht and was waiting at the airport when Elizabeth's plane touched down. He bounded nimbly up the aircraft steps to greet her—and stopped dead in amazement. Everywhere he looked he was confronted by a mass of heavily bearded faces. Everyone aboard the aircraft—even Elizabeth herself and her ladies-in-waiting—was sporting a false beard. Elizabeth had rented them in bulk from a London theatrical outfitter.

*

Only once has Elizabeth's impish sense of humor been displayed to the public. The occasion was a garden party at Buckingham Palace with several thousand guests clustered on the lawns eagerly awaiting the appearance of the royal family. First to appear was Elizabeth's mother—limping as the result of a fall on some steps at Windsor. Next came Philip—also limping, the result of a tumble at polo. Elizabeth thought it an opportunity too good to miss. "Limping seems to be the fashion this year," she joked— and feigned a limp as she too walked out into public view.

*

World War II found Elizabeth on the receiving end of one of her father's rare jokes. It was while she was serving in the Auxiliary Territorial Service. Wearing grease-stained overalls, she was working on the engine of a heavy truck the day her parents carried out a royal inspection of her unit; they decided to play a trick on her. While her mother engaged her in conversation, her father surreptitiously removed a small but vital part of the motor and popped it into his pocket. As a result, she was still struggling to get her truck started when the inspection ended. "What, not got it going yet?" her father chuckled.

*

Under heavy strain as he was, subject to constant ill health, Elizabeth's father, King George VI, was not a man much given to jokes. Indeed, Philip's frequent practical jokes sometimes irritated him. But he had his moments, and it was a joke that revealed the true courage of the man. Early in 1949 he underwent serious surgery that was to prolong his life another three years, and the surgeon, Professor James Learmouth, called regularly at the palace to check on his royal patient. On one such visit, to Learmouth's astonishment, the king suddenly produced a sword and waved it in his face. "You used a knife on me, Learmouth," he informed the startled surgeon. "Now I'm going to use one on you." His little joke over, the king instructed Learmouth to kneel, tapped him on the shoulder with the sword, and said, "Arise *Sir* James Learmouth."

*

Of Elizabeth's children, Charles and Andrew are the biggest jokers, though Anne, in childhood, was also fond of the occasional childish joke. Once on a visit to the Thames River Police, she was presented with a police whistle. It became her favorite joke to conceal herself in one of the shrubberies in the palace gardens, give a few loud blasts on her whistle, and watch the palace's protective policeman dash around trying to locate the source of the disturbance. Elizabeth's mother, on another occasion, returned from an afternoon stroll on the grounds at Sandringham to find her granddaughter trying to ride her pony up the front steps to the main door. It would be a great joke, Anne told her grandmother, to ride the pony right into the drawing room where her parents would be just about to sit down to afternoon tea. However, the pony had other ideas. All Anne's urgings and Granny's encouragement couldn't persuade it to mount the steps.

*

Andrew's favorite joke in childhood was to flit from room to room pressing the bell pushes intended for his mother's private use and then to vanish before a royal page appeared on the scene—just like kids who ring doorbells and then run away. As he grew older, his jokes became more elaborate. He once turned the fountain at Windsor Castle into a mass of foaming bubbles with a purloined packet of detergent. Another time, on the day of a royal garden party to which several thousand guests had been invited, he switched some of the specially erected direction signs so that people found themselves heading in all the wrong directions.

*

But what may be a joke with a child can be far from funny in a grown man, and Andrew's spray-painting incident in Los Angeles in 1984 did not go down at all well. It happened when Andrew visited a construction site in Watts. He picked up a spray gun for a closer look. "Don't squeeze the trigger," foreman Geary Cannon cautioned him. Andrew did not squeeze the trigger as he playfully threatened those around him with the paint-loaded weapon. Then he turned toward an open window where cameramen and reporters were clustered. This time he did squeeze the trigger, and the assembled press was sprayed with paint. "An accident," Andrew insisted. "I intended to paint the wall." Accident or joke, it had a costly outcome. Damage to cameras and clothes ran into several thousand dollars. One claim alone, from a photographer on the *Los Angeles Herald-Examiner*, was for $1,200. Buckingham Palace sent a banker's draft in settlement but refused to say whether Andrew himself had had to stump up. Given his mother's attitude toward money, the chances are that he did.

*

Whether the paint spraying was an accident, as Andrew claims, or his idea of a joke, it was certainly a case of like father, like son. Photographers trailing Philip during a visit to the Royal Chelsea Flower Show in London back in the 1950s were similarly sprayed with a jet of water operated by remote control at a time when he was being shown how the control system worked. Like Andrew, he has always insisted that it was not his fault—indeed, not his finger on the trigger. But the only two people with him at the time have similarly denied responsibility. So whose finger did the damage? Popular opinion at the time was best summed up by the man who joked, "I know Prince Philip didn't do it, but he shouldn't do it again."

*

Charles in childhood had a stuffed monkey almost as big as himself. One day, creeping unseen along an indoor balcony, he suddenly hurled it over the parapet, uttering a loud yell as he did so. Horrified servants in the hall below almost had heart failure, thinking for a moment that it was Charles himself hurtling down from the balcony.

Another childhood joke was the "whoopee cushion," so called because of the impolite noise it emits if anyone sits on it. On one occasion only prompt action on the part of an alert footman prevented a visiting bishop from falling victim to Charles' cushion.

Visiting Balmoral in the days when he was president, Dwight Eisenhower was amused to see the boy Charles wearing a homemade "I like Ike" badge. Another childhood joke took the form of an imitation inkblot that he would place in the middle of one of the valuable antique royal carpets.

Years later, with Charles now a young naval cadet, the inkblot gave way to some imitation dog dirt that Charles, in advance of a lecture, would leave in a conspicuous position on the floor of the lecture hall. The other cadets, as they filed in and took their seats, naturally stepped very carefully around this unpleasant-looking object. Enter Charles.

Instead of stepping around it, he would pause to inspect it, bend down and, to everyone's amazement, pick it up and pop it into his case along with his lecture notes.

*

Playing the fool "helps to keep me sane," Charles insists. His spell as a student at Cambridge University afforded him ample opportunity. Along with other students, he took part in a couple of amateur burlesque shows, appearing onstage in a variety of guises and delivering lines full of sexual innuendo. In one skit, for which he wore frogman's flippers and a gas mask, he was supposedly a TV weather forecaster. "By morning promiscuity will be widespread," he predicted. Another skit, in which he appeared as a cello-plucking pop star, saw him announced as "the biggest plucker in the business." In yet another he was a Victorian lecher intent on seducing a gypsy girl. "I like giving myself heirs," he leered as he bundled her offstage.

*

Nor could he resist playing the fool during a visit to the Canadian Arctic. It had been arranged for him to make a thirty-minute dive under the ice at Resolute Bay. Wearing an orange-colored suit filled with warm air, he duly made the dive. Then, clambering out again onto the ice, he promptly proceeded to inflate the suit to enormous proportions until he ended up looking like, in his own words, "a great orange walrus."

*

Another princely trip took him to Germany, to visit the Royal Regiment of Wales, of which he is colonel-in-chief. While there, he posed the time-honored question: "Any complaints?" There was one complaint. Shortage of girl-friends. It was difficult to pick up girls when you didn't speak German, the Welsh soldiers explained. Shortly after

Charles' visit, they were surprised to receive a handbook of German phrases designed to help them in their amorous designs on the local frauleins. Their princely colonel-in-chief had sat down on his return home and compiled it for them.

*

There were some hilarious high jinks at sea during Charles' years in the navy. "I'll send you all to the Tower of London," he threatened his fellow officers on one ship. The fact that he was the ship's communications officer at the time afforded facilities to put his threat into effect. Arriving back in Britain and due for a spot of shore leave, his fellow officers found waiting for them at the dockside a conveyance labeled in large letters: "HM Tower of London for Officers of HMS Jupiter."

Not that the joking aboard ship was all one way. It was Charles' job one day to inflate and release balloons being used for gunnery practice. He had already released several and was busy inflating another when he realized that what he had in his hand was not a target balloon but a contraceptive device.

He was less easily caught out the night there was an attempt to debag him during a skylarking party in the officers' wardroom. Guessing that something of the sort might happen, he arrived suitably prepared. Off came his trousers—only to reveal a second pair beneath. Off came those, too—to reveal yet a third pair.

His farewell party when he quit the navy after a brief period of command saw him pushed ashore in a battered wheelchair with a lavatory seat slung around his neck. Overhead fluttered a banner bearing the words: "Command Has Aged Me." "Keep your bowels open, Sir" was the parting advice of the ship's medic as he made the farewell presentation—a roll of toilet paper.

*

Charles himself has a fair way with words. During his brief spell as a naval skipper he greeted a beauty queen who visited his ship: "I hope you've taken the pill this morning." A look of consternation came over her face. "The seasickness pill, I mean," added Charles, grinning.

Actress Susan Hampshire was presented to him at a charity show. She was wearing a decidedly low-cut gown. Charles told her: "My father said that if ever I met a lady in a dress like yours, I must look her straight in the eyes or someone might take a photograph of me in what might appear to be a compromising position."

For a trip to the Canadian Arctic he was swaddled in caribou fur. "I hope we don't meet a polar bear," he joked. "He might think I'm in season."

*

Charles is fond of riddles, too. A favorite one is: "How do you tell a worm's head from its tail? Put it in a saucer of flour and wait till it coughs."

But princely jokes can sometimes backfire. In one of the many speeches he made when he and Diana were in Australia Charles joked that they were raising William on a diet of warm milk and minced kangaroo meat in the hope of ensuring that he was a bonny, *bouncing* boy. Some people didn't get the joke, and there were complaints that kangaroo meat was not suitable for such a young child (William was under a year at the time). Charles sought to put things right. "It was meant as a joke," he explained in a subsequent speech—and could not resist making another. "In fact, we are bringing William up on a diet of grass and beer."

*

Diana is less jokey than Charles, though a gag he pulled during a charity show at London's Royal Opera House found her responsive enough. Slipping unnoticed from his seat in the royal box, Charles suddenly appeared onstage, a comic figure in tights and tunic. To the delight of the audience, he proceeded to play a mock Romeo and Juliet scene with Diana, still in the royal box. "Speak to me, speak to me," he implored in tones of mock passion. Entering into the spirit of things, Diana leaned out toward him and warbled, "Just one cornetto," the catch phrase of an ice-cream commercial seen on British television. Nor was the joke yet at an end. Charles dashed offstage and returned with a ladder, which he propped against the royal box, scaling it to seize his wife's hand and kiss his way up her arm.

Upstairs, Downstairs

Buckingham Palace is like a small, separate township in the very heart of London, complete with its own post office and telephone exchange, police and fire stations, repair shops, filling station, carpenter's and blacksmith's shops, its own pharmacy and sick bay, and its own "village store" selling everything from canned fruit to candy, from packets of tea to cans of beer. The two-acre site on which the palace stands is without doubt the most valuable piece of real estate in London—and there are a further forty acres of gardens to go with it. So huge is the place that there are servants who never get to see Elizabeth or Philip from one year's end to the next; there are parts of the palace Elizabeth herself has never penetrated in all her years of monarchy. It has its own picture gallery and movie theater as well as a ballroom and swimming pool. The ballroom is 123 feet long, 60 feet wide, and 45 feet high from floor to gilded ceiling. The picture gallery is longer—150 feet—and the crimson-carpeted corridor at the front of the palace longer still, an enormous 240 feet. Everything is big. Even the state dining table, when fully extended, stretches a staggering 80 feet.

The palace contains miles of corridor, enormous gilded state rooms in which Elizabeth hosts visiting monarchs and presidents, dimly lit offices in which royal aides toil diligently, a vast subterranean basement, cozy self-contained apartments for top servants, and a range of bed-sitters for those lower down. No one knows for certain how many rooms there are in the place. "I haven't a clue," Diana said frankly in Australia. Philip once set about counting them and got lost in the process. "Sorry, I thought this was the post office," he apologized to two surprised maids when he barged into their rest room by mistake. His final room count made the total 611, but it depends on what you call a room. Some of the closets are so big they could serve an ordinary family as a living room, while folding glass doors enable stretches of corridor to become separate rooms on occasion. Certainly there are enough rooms to warrant over five hundred fireplaces, three hundred clocks, nearly as many telephones, and a squad of mailmen who go from room to room delivering letters.

*

The palace stands on the site of a former pleasure garden that in the seventeenth century was haunted by prostitutes and the young rakes of the day. Before that it was a mulberry orchard. King James I planted the mulberry trees with the idea of breeding silkworms and starting a silk industry. But he planted the wrong sort of tree, and the worms never bred. One of those original mulberry trees still grows in the palace gardens.

*

Its royal residents have seldom had a kind word to say about the palace. Queen Victoria complained that it was too small, and King Edward VII styled it "a sepulchre." Elizabeth's grandfather, King George V, would have much preferred to live at Kensington Palace (where Charles and Diana now live when in London). The Duke of Windsor thought it "dank and musty," while Elizabeth's father found it "an icebox." Elizabeth, when she became queen, wanted to stay on in her old home, Clarence House, but prime minister Winston Churchill insisted that a queen must live in a palace. So she changed residences with her mother.

*

Elizabeth and Philip occupy only a very small part of the palace, a mere sixteen of its six hundred-plus rooms. Their apartment is on the second floor, a fact that enables Philip to joke, "We live over the shop." It includes a large bay-windowed sitting room that also does duty as Elizabeth's study, a separate study for Philip, their private dining room, their bedroom, a bathroom and a dressing room each, and a room that serves as a kennel for the corgis and dorgis. The rooms all interconnect.

Elizabeth and Philip sleep in a large double bed amid a flurry of filmy draperies suspended from a gilt crown. No page or footman is allowed to enter the royal bedroom—only maids—though Philip's valet is permitted into his bathroom and dressing room. The footman who brings Philip his early-morning pot of tea leaves it on a table in the corridor outside. Elizabeth's personal maid collects it from there and takes it into the bedroom.

*

Philip also has a bed in his dressing room which he some-times uses to avoid disturbing Elizabeth if he is out late or needs to be up and away early. It was because he had slept separately and left early that Elizabeth was alone in the royal bedroom when she awoke just after dawn one morning to find a strange man sitting on the side of her bed.

The stranger was barefoot. In one hand he held part of a broken glass ashtray. Blood dripped from his hand onto the bed cover from where he had cut himself. His name was Michael Fagan.

107

The incident revealed great gaps in the royal security system. The intruder had entered the palace by scaling a drainpipe to an open window. A servant who saw him wandering along one of the red-carpeted corridors thought he was a workman and failed to raise the alarm. The security man guarding the door of the royal bedroom had gone off duty and his relief had not arrived. The footman who should also have been on duty was walking the corgis in the garden. When Elizabeth triggered her alarm button, whoever was on duty in the palace police station thought the system had simply gone on the blink and ignored it.

Displaying considerable coolness, Elizabeth asked Fagan if he would like a cigarette. When he said he would, she used it as an excuse to ring for her maid, Elizabeth Andrews.

By this time footman Paul Whybrew had returned from walking the corgis. While Elizabeth climbed out of bed and donned her robe, Whybrew and Elizabeth Andrews encouraged Fagan to go into another room, where they gave him some whiskey and sent for the police.

Fagan gave various rambling reasons for entering the palace. "I am in love with Elizabeth Regina," he said at one stage. "I wanted to prove that security was lax; that the queen was not safe," he said another time. He certainly proved that all right.

In addition to showing up the inadequacy of the royal security system (considerably tightened up since), the incident also revealed a curious gap in Britain's legal system. Because Fagan had not actually broken into the palace but had gained entry through an open window, he could not be charged with a criminal offense.

*

Unlike the White House, there are no guided tours to Buckingham Palace. The taxpayers who pay for its upkeep get to see inside only if they are among the privileged few hundred invited to investitures (when Elizabeth distributes medals, knighthoods, and other honors) or the few thousand invited to royal garden parties. The best the ordinary tourist can hope for is to see a small exhibition of royal paintings displayed in an annex known as the Queen's Gallery or, on certain afternoons in summer, to be allowed to browse among the coaches, carriages, and horses in the royal mews. Neither excursion will actually get them inside the palace proper, and they have to pay for the privilege. But anyone can telephone the palace. The number is listed in the London telephone book. But no one gets through to Elizabeth or any of her family unless they know the appropriate code word.

*

Elizabeth herself has a telephone chat with her mother before starting work each day. A direct line links their two residences. There is a similar direct line between Buckingham Palace and Kensington Palace, Charles and Diana's London residence. Outside calls are never dialed by Elizabeth herself. Someone else does that for her, getting through to whoever it is she wishes to contact before she herself comes on the line. So it came as a surprise to a servant, answering the telephone at Sandringham on one occasion, to hear a voice announce, "This is the queen speaking." The servant thought himself the victim of a practical joke. "Now pull the other leg," he chortled. "But this really is the queen," the voice persisted. "I need help." She was stranded, her car bogged down in a snowdrift. She had abandoned it, tramped across a snow-covered field, and was calling from a convenient cottage.

*

Royal aides advise and assist Elizabeth in her work as monarch; royal servants run the palace—and there is a

109

clear-cut social division between the two. Curiously, though they do no domestic work, the aides are known collectively and officially as the Queen's Household. Reference books list some four hundred of them, but the validity of such lists can be judged from the fact that they include the name of Princess Margaret's one-time beau, Peter Townsend, who has not been inside the palace for thirty years. Others on the list, with quaint old-world titles such as Gold Stick, Gentleman Usher of the Black Rod, and Gentlemen at Arms, perform only occasional ceremonial duties, and some, like Townsend, none at all. The list includes a poet laureate, whose task it is to pen a few verses on occasions such as Charles and Diana's wedding, and a Keeper of the Swans, whose post is a hangover from the days when swans were bred for the royal dining table. What are known as Ladies and Women of the Bedchamber (though most people term them ladies-in-waiting) do actually work for Elizabeth part-time. They take turns attending her for two weeks at a time, answering correspondence and accompanying her to her public engagements. They are unpaid for this and do it largely for the honor of the thing, though they do get a dress allowance. Of the four hundred-odd names officially listed, only about sixty—private secretaries, press secretaries, accountants, stenographers, and the like—actually work for Elizabeth on a full-time, salaried basis.

On the other hand, servants who actually do the household work are not regarded as members of the Queen's Household. There are over three hundred of them, mostly full-time, some part-time. They include ten pages, twelve footmen, three dressers to take care of Elizabeth's clothes, two valets to look after Philip's, two dozen housemaids, the same number of cleaning women, twelve underbutlers, four electricians, three carpenters, three upholsterers, two plumbers, and a french polisher. In the kitchens, in addition to the royal chef, there are special pastry chefs and a number of underchefs who cook only for other servants. In the mews to the rear of the palace there are about fifty grooms, chauffeurs, coachmen, and motor mechanics along with a blacksmith to shoe the horses. There are also twelve porters for the heavy work of fetching and carrying, a squad of men who clean the hundreds of windows nonstop, and a man who comes in each week to spend two–three days winding the three hundred palace clocks.

*

Many of the servants live at the palace. Chauffeurs and grooms live above the garages and stables in the mews. Top servants such as the steward and the housekeeper have three-room apartments in the palace itself. Footmen and maids have cozy bed-sitters in what were once the attics, maids at the front of the palace and footmen at the rear.

Philip was horrified, when he and Elizabeth first moved into the palace, at the conditions in which some servants lived, huddled together in attic cubicles made from matchboard. "Horse boxes," Philip called them and ordered them gutted. In their place are now cozy ranges of bed-sitters, each with its own bed, wardrobe, chest of drawers, easy chair, and wash basin. Maids also have a dressing table apiece and footmen a writing table.

It was Philip, too, who put a stop to the outmoded tradition of pages and footmen powdering their hair so that it looked snow-white. The "powder" was in fact a mixture of flour and starch, and the whole business was incredibly messy. It was also unmanly, Philip thought, and ordered it stopped. Or at least Elizabeth did on her husband's suggestion.

But pages and footmen are still required to don old-fashioned outfits of tunic, knee breeches, and buckled shoes for state occasions such as the visit of President and Mrs. Reagan.

111

In addition to accommodating many of her servants, Elizabeth also feeds them. So palace housekeeping is on a mammoth scale. Daily deliveries include eight huge churns of milk, one hundred loaves of bread, twenty-four dozen eggs, and 120 pounds of potatoes.

Still working at the palace as this book was written was Elizabeth's oldest, most loyal, and most favored servant. As a servant, Margaret MacDonald does not rank as one of the Queen's Household, but her position of trust and confidence is second to none in the royal hierarchy. Now in her seventies, she has been with Elizabeth—as nursery-maid, nanny, personal maid, and dresser—since she was in her late teens and Elizabeth a new-born baby princess. Over the years she has become almost like a second mother to the queen. While other palace servants address Elizabeth as "Your Majesty" and even top aides call her "Ma'am," she is "Lilibet" to Margaret MacDonald. In return, the queen calls her "Bobo." The name stems from childhood games of hide-and-seek and the excited little shrieks of "Boo ... boo" with which servant and toddling princess would surprise one another.

Daughter of a Scottish railroad worker, Bobo has been with Elizabeth at all the high spots of her life. It was to her that Elizabeth first confided that she was in love with Philip. She helped Elizabeth into her dress on her wedding day and again, a few years later, into her coronation gown. She was with her in Kenya when word was received that Elizabeth's father was dead and that she was now Queen Elizabeth II. She has since traveled the world with Elizabeth, seeing to her packing, masterminding her wardrobe, ensuring her comfort. She has been indefatigable in duty and loyalty, rarely taking a day off, steering clear of marriage in order to devote herself entirely to Elizabeth. There was one occasion, with Elizabeth due to make an overseas tour, when it seemed that Bobo was too ill to go with her. Doggedly, she refused to remain behind and had herself carried aboard the royal yacht on a stretcher.

*

Elizabeth dotes on Bobo, and her years of loyal service have not gone unrewarded. She has many gifts Elizabeth has given her, including a pearl necklace, and she alone among palace servants possesses the Royal Victorian Order, a decoration Elizabeth awards only for special personal services. She has her own apartment at Buckingham Palace, her meals are specially prepared by Elizabeth's own royal chef, and there is a royal car at her disposal for outings. All this places her in a very special category among royal servants. To other servants, she is always "Mrs. MacDonald" (though she is not married), and a newly arrived footman who once referred to her as "Bobo" received an immediate rebuke. "Only the queen calls me that," she told him.

Because of her age, she no longer travels with Elizabeth. But with two assistant dressers to help her, she continues to mastermind Elizabeth's wardrobe, which is so vast that it occupies three large rooms at the palace. While other royal servants retire around the age of sixty, Bobo has no thought of retiring while Elizabeth still has need of her. "She won't leave the palace until they carry her out" is the opinion of other royal servants.

*

Philip, when he first married Elizabeth, was inclined to resent the close and sometimes cloying relationship between her and Bobo, and his decision to send Charles away to school was partly to avert the possibility of a similar close relationship developing between the boy prince and his nanny. So Charles' nanny was abruptly pensioned off and Charles himself packed off to boarding school. At the time, Charles was very upset at being parted from his nanny. He soon got over it, as boys do, but never forgot her. Years later, when the time came for him to be invested as Prince of Wales at Caernarvon Castle, he saw to it that his old nanny had a seat at the ceremony.

*

Demarcation—that sickness from which much of British industry has suffered for so long—is also to be found at Buckingham Palace, and has been ever since Queen Victoria's day. Elizabeth's great-great-grandmother once instructed the Master of the Household to have a fire lit in the royal sitting room. To her amazement, he replied that, with due respect, it was not his job, Your Majesty. It was the job of the Lord Steward. So Queen Victoria made her request to the Lord Steward, and the fire was duly laid. Laid, but not lighted. Lighting the fire, the Lord Steward told the queen, was the responsibility of the Lord Chamberlain. Things are better today, but not much. If Elizabeth rings for a servant, it is a page's job to answer the summons. If the page on duty is temporarily not available, she can ring until she is blue in the face and no one will appear. While several footmen may hear the bell, they won't answer. Similarly, a page will not clean royal shoes. That is a job for a footman. And the footmen, though they clean shoes, will not polish the silver. That is a job for an underbutler. Nor will they draw the curtains when dusk falls. That is for the maids to do.

*

Unlike Britain's miners, shipworkers, and carmakers, royal servants have never actually gone on strike. The nearest they ever came to striking was a sit-in at the servants' hall at the palace. Cause of the dispute—food. Served cold meat and salad for the third day running, they threatened to stay where they were in the dining hall until they got something hot. A supply of fried eggs and french fries was quickly rustled up, and the dispute was over.

*

On balance, Elizabeth is a considerate, even generous, employer. At Balmoral Castle each summer she throws a party called the Gillies' Ball for her Scottish staff and those from London who are there with her. She, Philip, and any others of the family who are there at the time join in the festivities, donning full Highland regalia for the occasion, whooping and hollering with the rest as the dancing heats up to the music of the bagpipes. At Buckingham Palace, ahead of Christmas, she stages another dance for her servants, with a top-name band hired to play for them. At Christmas she buys a gift for every servant, socks and pantyhose for newcomers, more expensive gifts—tea sets, coffee sets, traveling clocks—for those who have been with her longer. Really senior servants—housekeeper, steward, sergeant footman, and the royal chef—can select their own gifts from a prepared list. Philip and others of the family help her to distribute the gifts. One year, intrigued by a new coffee-making gadget intended for one of the footmen, Philip could not resist dismantling it to see how it worked. He then found out that he could not get it together again. "Here, see what you can do," he told the footman, handing over the bits. "If you can't get it to work, get another and charge it to me."

*

Like many others in today's Britain, some royal servants augment their normal wages by moonlighting, taking casual work elsewhere in their off-duty hours. Royal housemaids sometimes act as cloakroom girls for functions at foreign embassies. Royal chauffeurs have been known to drive for private hire firms. Pages and footmen act as waiters and butlers at society functions. Indeed, there has been the rare occasion when Elizabeth has gone along to a dinner party to find herself being waited upon by a face familiar to her at Buckingham Palace.

*

And like the royals themselves, palace servants indulge in the occasional spate of high jinks and practical joking. Footmen, clearing up after a state banquet on one occasion, indulged in rather too much leftover champagne and ended up squirting each other with soda syphons to the detriment of their expensive liveries. A favorite practical joke among servants is reserved for occasions of high ceremony, such as royal weddings, when members of the family traditionally make an appearance on Buckingham Palace's famous balcony. While the royals are readying themselves for their public appearance, some joker among the servants will creep along and twitch the curtains that screen the glass doors leading to the balcony. A great roar immediately goes up from the vast crowd gathered in front of the palace, who think this heralds the appearance of the royal family, and behind the scenes, royal servants have a good laugh at public expense.

Royal Duty

Elizabeth II is queen not only of Great Britain and Northern Ireland but of seventeen other countries, among them Canada, Australia, and New Zealand. In addition, she is recognized as Head of the Commonwealth in almost twice that number of former British colonies that are now independent republics.

*

In Britain she is theoretically all-powerful. On paper she can:

- dismiss the prime minister
- do away with Parliament
- disband the army
- sell off the ships of the navy
- declare war on another country
- give parts of Britain to the United States (or anyone else)
- pardon and release all convicted criminals
- make anyone in Britain a lord or lady

*

All this, in twentieth-century Britain, is the merest fiction, of course, part and parcel of the ancient monarchy myth. In reality, Elizabeth has very little real power, though she may have considerable influence. The last British monarch who actually dismissed a prime minister was King William IV, and that was 150 years ago. Today, Elizabeth—and Charles when he takes over—can do only what Parliament decrees or the prime minister of the day advises. The wide gap between myth and reality results in a curious anomaly. While tradition still insists that no parliamentary bill becomes the law of the land without Elizabeth's royal assent, she cannot refuse to give such assent indefinitely. The third time she is asked, she must sign anything Parliament puts before her—even if it is her own abdication.

*

To preserve the fiction that Elizabeth II is all-powerful, Britain's prime minister and others of the Government also belong to the Privy Council, a circle of wiseacres who "advise" the queen when she makes decisions. The Privy Council meets, on average, once every two weeks, and its meetings are quaint in the extreme. Everyone, including Elizabeth herself, remains standing throughout. New members (and there can be several when a new government takes over) are sworn in on their hands and knees. Even Elizabeth herself had a job not to laugh the day one batch of newcomers, finding themselves down on their hands and knees in the wrong part of the room, obsequiously crawled on all fours to the correct spot. "Pure mumbo jumbo," one former president of the council once styled the whole business.

*

Elizabeth also has a number of top aides to ease her through the complexities of monarchy. The senior of these top aides rejoices in the old-world title of Lord Chamberlain. He masterminds royal ceremonies such as Charles and Diana's wedding and, among other things, has the delicate task of ensuring that ladies admitted to the royal enclosure at Ascot races are wearing both hats and dresses (not trousers). Two symbols of his authority make him easily identified on such state occasions as the royal banquet given at Windsor Castle to welcome President and Mrs. Reagan to Britain. One is the gold key slung at his waist; the other is the white staff he carries in his hand. When Elizabeth dies, as his last act of service to her, he will break the staff in two and cast the pieces into the burial vault.

*

The bulk of Elizabeth's workload splits neatly into two categories. There are public appearances at home and overseas, with which others of the family help out. Then there is the paperwork with which no one else, not even Philip, is permitted to help. She calls it "doing my boxes." The phrase derives from the fact that the state papers she is required to sign by Parliament and the other seventeen countries of which she is also queen reach her in a seemingly nonstop succession of rectangular boxes covered in red, green, or black leather.

*

Elizabeth tackles the contents of her boxes in her spacious, comfortable sitting room on the second floor of Buckingham Palace, sitting at a flat-topped antique desk set in the bay window so that she can look out to the garden. The top of the desk is so cluttered as to be almost invisible. Jostling for space on it are two telephones, a desk lamp, a dozen family photographs, a blotting pad, a rack holding scarlet-crested stationery, a rotary calendar, a brass carriage clock, a gilt-framed list of the day's appointments, a loose-leaf diary of future engagements, a tray for documents and correspondence, a scribbling pad, a paste

119

pot, pencils, paper clips, rubber bands, a moist sponge (so that she can seal envelopes without licking them), wax candle and matches (for impressing her royal seal where required), and three letter openers, one gold, one jeweled, one plastic. She usually uses the plastic one.

*

Elizabeth's mail averages 120 letters a day. They are sorted for her by her page. Code words on the envelopes indicate pesonal letters from relatives and friends, and these he leaves for Elizabeth to open herself. Others go to her aides to deal with, though she will see them all in due course, with the possible exception of those from cranks. One woman wrote to her for years claiming that she was the true queen of England and Elizabeth a usurper.

There are frequently letters from people who regard her as a court of last resort. One such was from the father of a girl due to marry a soldier. The wedding date had already been changed once because of the soldier's military duties. When further military duties necessitated a second change, the bride's father appealed to Elizabeth. "I have to pay the bills and can't afford to keep changing the date," he wrote. She passed the letter on to the Secretary for Defence. While officially she cannot interfere in such matters, the mere fact that they have been brought to her attention is often sufficient to get things put right. In the case of the soldier, his orders were changed so that the wedding could go ahead.

*

If Elizabeth is theoretically all-powerful, Philip is the opposite. "Constitutionally I don't exist," he says himself. He is down on the royal payroll merely as "husband of the queen." Husband or not, prince or not, he is not permitted to see the contents of Elizabeth's boxes (though Charles, as heir to the throne, can). Nor is he allowed to be present when his wife and Britain's prime minister confer on matters of state. A man accustomed to giving orders rather than taking them, this absence of authority caused him to be very frustrated and depressed in the early years of his wife's reign. "I feel like a glorified lodger," he lamented once. But he has gotten used to it since, creating his own sphere of authority in other directions.

*

Philip has his own study five doors along from Elizabeth. If hers is more of a sitting room than a study, cozy and feminine, his is a push-button paradise. Television, tape recorder, even the curtains hanging at the windows, can all be operated by remote control.

*

Elizabeth and Philip send out around six hundred Christmas cards each year to the few other monarchs left in today's world, to presidents and prime ministers, ambassadors and church dignitaries, relatives and friends. Not for them cards adorned with holly and robins. A family photograph is more their style. They both sign the whole six hundred personally. It was once suggested to Elizabeth that she should have a rubber-stamp signature made for Christmas cards and official photographs. She refused. "It won't mean the same if they are not signed personally," she said. She herself gets thousands of cards each Christmas, mostly from people she has never even heard of. Cards with horses on them are her particular favorite, and they clutter the royal mantelpiece over Christmas.

*

Elizabeth's training as a future queen started when her uncle abdicated in order to marry Mrs. Simpson and her father became king in his place. She was ten. Childlike, she said that when she became queen she would pass a law forbidding people to ride horses on Sundays. "Horses need a rest, too," she said. She has learned since that it is Parliament, not kings or queens, who make laws, and her no-riding-on-Sundays regulation has never come about.

As part of her training, a special picture book was compiled to teach Elizabeth about monarchy. She was made to study the life of Queen Victoria, to learn French, German, and Latin, to study the histories of Britain, Europe, and the United States. Once a week her grandmother, Queen Mary, took her on visits to places like the Tower of London, the British Museum, the Bank of England, the National Gallery, and the Royal Mint. Crowds often gathered to see the small girl who would one day be queen. "Have all these people come just to see me?" she asked on one occasion. The remark so shocked her grandmother that she took Elizabeth straight home again.

At twelve Elizabeth began to travel back and forth to Eton College, Britain's most exclusive boys' school, for lessons in constitutional history. Not that she ever met any of the boys. She was the only child in a class of one. At fourteen she made her first radio broadcast, at sixteen she became an honorary colonel in the Grenadier Guards, and by eighteen she was a full-fledged princess, hosting visiting prime ministers, visiting U.S. airbases in wartime Britain, and standing in for her father when he was out of the country.

*

As Elizabeth's eldest son, Charles will be Britain's next king. He has known that from the age of four when, as his first lesson in future kingship, he was taken to Westminster Abbey to see his mother crowned. Anne, being younger and more of a chatterbox, had to stay behind at the palace. Not long after, the two of them stood together at a window, watching the guard being changed in the palace forecourt.

"Oh, look," said Anne as the soldiers of the guard marched to and fro. "It's another coronation."

"No, it isn't," said Charles. "There won't be another coronation for years and years and years, and then it will be mine."

*

Charles has learned about kingship, he says, "the way a monkey learns—by watching its parents." He watched and imitated to such good purpose that within months of his mother's coronation he was already greeting visitors to Buckingham Palace with a childish handshake. Handshaking became so much a part of his childhood that he even went to shake hands with his mother when she returned home after an absence of six months on her coronation world tour. "Oh, no, not you," Elizabeth sighed, sweeping him into her arms and kissing him.

*

At five, as one of his Christmas presents, Charles was given a velvet cloak and a miniature sword. He used the sword to practice bestowing "knighthoods" on two of the palace footmen. Later, like his mother before him, he was taken to visit places like Westminster Abbey, the Tower of London, and the Science Museum. To improve his French, he was permitted to speak only French at mealtimes. He was sent each week to a private gymnasium to toughen him. Then, to make him tougher still, Philip suggested buzzing him off to boarding school.

Charles was the first heir to the throne in history ever to go to boarding school. At school, he was set to make his own bed, wait on other boys at mealtimes, and even hump garbage bins to the collection point. At nine he was created Prince of Wales (though his ceremonial investiture was not for another eleven years). By eighteen, though still at school, he was deputizing for his mother when she was out of the country. But he was not asked for his views, was not even present, when a top-level conference was held at the palace to plan his future training program. Out of that conference came the plan to send him to university, then to the Royal Naval College at Dartmouth, and then into the navy for five years, all of which he did.

*

Andrew's training, because he was never heir to the throne, has been less stylized. For generations it has been a royal family tradition that second sons go into the navy. Queen Victoria's second son, Alfred, was thirty-five years in the navy. King Edward VII's second son, George, was twenty years in the navy and quit with reluctance when the death of his elder brother obliged him to take over as Prince of Wales and later King George V. His second son, in turn, Elizabeth's father, was made to join the navy at thirteen, fought at the Battle of Jutland during World War I, and was disappointed when he was invalided out with duodenal ulcers.

In Andrew's case, there is also a strong naval tradition on the other side of his family tree. His paternal great-grandfather was a German princeling who left Germany at the age of fourteen to become a British citizen and join the British navy. His son, Andrew's great-uncle, was Earl Mountbatten of Burma, skipper of the destroyer *Kelly* until it was dive-bombed and sunk with the loss of 130 lives during World War II. Mountbatten himself was rescued from the sea to become Supreme Commander in South East Asia and was still wearing his old *Kelly* sweater the day he was murdered by the IRA at the age of seventy-nine. And Andrew's father, Prince Philip, was decorated for bravery following the Battle of Cape Matapan during World War II when Britain's Mediterranean fleet sank four

Italian cruisers and two destroyers without sustaining a single casualty.

*

It was Andrew's turn to prove his mettle when Argentina invaded the Falkland Islands. When Britain's hastily improvised battle fleet sailed to recapture the islands, Andrew went with it. His mother could have intervened to prevent his going, but that is not her way. Said a statement issued on her behalf, "He is a serving officer, and there is no question that he should go. Neither operational requirements, nor indeed Prince Andrew himself, would tolerate him being singled out for special treatment."

His princely locks cropped to combat length, Andrew flew his helicopter around the clock, rescuing men from the sea when British ships were sunk, ferrying supplies between ships, taking supplies to troops ashore on the islands, acting as a decoy to divert incoming Exocet missiles from hitting the carrier *Invincible*. Andrew himself explains: "The idea is that the Exocet comes in low and is not supposed to get above a height of twenty-seven feet. So, when the missile is coming at you, you rise quickly above twenty-seven feet and it flies harmlessly underneath." That, at least, is the theory. "But on the day the *Sheffield* was hit," Andrew recalls, "one Exocet flew over the mast—and that's well above twenty-seven feet."

The British task force's own Sea Wolf missiles, he found, were almost as great a hazard as the enemy Exocets. "Sea Wolves locked onto our helicopter three times while we were hovering," Andrew remembers. "It's not much fun having one of those pick you out as a target. That really makes the hair stand up on the back of your head."

*

With the birth of children to Charles and Diana, Andrew is no longer second in the line of succession to the throne. He was at birth, though Anne was older. Sexual equality cuts no ice when it comes to being king or queen in Britain. Sons rank ahead of daughters; brothers, even younger brothers, ahead of sisters. Elizabeth would never have become queen if she had had a younger brother. He would have been king instead. And had Diana's first child been a girl instead of a boy, she would have become queen sometime in the future only if her parents did not have a son later. Before William was born, when no one knew whether the baby would be a boy or a girl, some politicians sought to have the law changed so that Charles and Diana's firstborn child, of whichever sex, would be the future monarch. With a queen on the throne and Margaret Thatcher as prime minister, you might have thought that the proposal stood a good chance of becoming law. Curiously, neither Elizabeth nor Mrs. Thatcher was in favor of it, and the whole business fizzled out.

So the order of succession to the throne remains as it has been for a thousand years. It descends vertically through the eldest son in the first instance, with males taking precedence over females, and horizontally through brothers and sisters only if the vertical line is at an end. At present, the order is:

1. Charles
2. His son, William
3. His second son, Henry

With the vertical line of inheritance then at an end, it goes on:

4. Andrew
5. Edward
6. Anne
7. Anne's son, Peter Phillips
8. Anne's daughter, Zara Phillips
9. Margaret
10. Margaret's son, David, Viscount Linley

11. Margaret's daughter, Lady Sarah Armstrong-Jones

Any other children Charles and Diana may have will rank ahead of Andrew. Andrew's children (if he marries and has children) will rank ahead of Edward, and Edward's children will rank ahead of Anne and her children.

There are over forty others in the full line of succession, including Elizabeth's cousins, the Gloucesters, the Kents, and the Harewoods, as well as the King and Crown Prince of Norway, five Rumanian princesses, and two Yugoslavian princes who can trace their ancestry back to the royal family tree.

*

The moment a British monarch dies, the heir becomes king or queen. Hence the expression "The king is dead. Long live the king." Elizabeth herself became queen under curious circumstances. When her father died, she was several thousand miles away, wearing slacks and a shirt and perched in the branches of a giant fig tree, feeding bananas to a troop of baboons. The fig tree was in Kenya's Aberdare Forest. Its huge branches cradled a treehouse from which Elizabeth and Philip were studying and filming the local wildlife. That was in 1952. Thirty-one years later, in 1983, Elizabeth made a sentimental journey back to the spot. She found it much changed. The small treehouse that had been her first royal residence had been destroyed by fire. In its place, because so many tourists now visit the spot where she became queen, stands a large hotel.

*

Elizabeth's father, King George VI, died at the family's country home, Sandringham. So did his father before him, King George V. In George V's day the clocks at Sandringham were always set half an hour ahead of the rest of

Britain. "Sandringham time," Elizabeth's grandfather called it. The idea was to get everybody out of bed half an hour earlier so that the king could get in an extra half hour's pheasant shooting. Not everyone shared the king's enthusiasm for being up and about early. His eldest son, the Duke of Windsor, certainly did not. Even as his father lay dying, he summoned a local clockmaker and ordered him to set all the clocks in the house to the correct time. By the time the job was done King George V was dead and Windsor was King Edward VIII.

*

Though King George V died at Sandringham, the state funeral took place in London, with the body later interred in the royal vault at Windsor. The coffin was borne through London on a gun carriage. On top of the coffin rested the royal crown. Pacing immediately behind came the new King Edward VIII and his three brothers. As the gun carriage rattled over a grating, the coffin jolted, dislodging the cross that surmounts the crown. The crown fell to the ground. As one of the accompanying military escort quickly scooped it up, the new king murmured to his brothers, "That's an unlucky omen." And so it proved. In less than a year he was king no more.

*

When Elizabeth II arrived back in London as Britain's new queen, she found her eighty-four-year-old grandmother, Queen Mary, waiting to greet her. "I wanted your old granny to be the first of your subjects to kiss your hand, Your Majesty," said the old lady as she knelt to her granddaughter just as Elizabeth in childhood had once knelt to her.

*

With Elizabeth, work comes first. In the early days of her monarchy there were sometimes spats between her and Philip because he wanted her to drop things to watch him play polo and she would not. On vacation at Balmoral Castle, she will breakfast in riding kit but move to her desk and tackle the contents of her boxes—they pursue her wherever she goes—before she actually goes riding. Even the sinusitis from which she suffered at one time, though it obliged her to cancel a number of public engagements, was not permitted to interfere with her paperwork. Confined to bed though she was, she had the boxes taken to her bedroom. Even when Andrew and Edward were born, she permitted herself only one day off. The day before each of them was born found her working away at her desk, and the day after she was working again, sitting up in bed, her box beside her.

*

She can be extremely obstinate where what she regards as her royal duty is concerned. The sinusitis by which she was plagued for so long reached its peak on a day of pelting rain. It was also the day of her annual birthday parade, a ceremony that requires her to ride sidesaddle for an hour or more at the head of her guards. Ill as she had been for six months or more with a succession of heavy colds, royal aides thought her in no condition to perform the traditional ceremony in such weather. Concerned for her, Philip added his plea. "Postpone it," he suggested. Elizabeth took him to a window and pointed down to hundreds of would-be spectators massed outside the palace, huddled under umbrellas and plastic hoods. "If they can stand the rain, then so can I. I won't disappoint them," she insisted.

*

She was just the same when she found herself unexpectedly pregnant with Andrew. Pregnancy could

129

hardly have come at a worse time. She was thirty-three and about to embark on the longest tour of Canada she had ever undertaken, a coast-to-coast trek scheduled to last just two days short of seven weeks. Her physicians suggested canceling the trip or at least abridging it. Elizabeth refused, refused even to have anyone in Canada told of her condition. And off she went, taking along an extra needlewoman, whose job it was to alter her dresses as tour and pregnancy progressed. Despite the pangs of morning sickness, she struggled through days of public engagements that started sometimes at eight in the morning and continued until after midnight; endured temperatures that one day in Toronto soared to ninety-five degrees. A side trip to Chicago meant a thirteen-hour day during which she visited the Art Institute, the Museum of Science and Industry, and a trade fair, inspected an honor guard and, with her teeth troubling her, also crammed in a visit to a local dentist. There were times when she nearly collapsed, and she was so exhausted when she reached the Yukon that Philip had to go to Yellowknife and Dawson City alone. But Elizabeth, after a day in bed, insisted on getting up again next morning and setting off on a four-day whistle-stop tour of the prairie provinces.

*

In addition to visiting the various countries of which she is queen, Elizabeth also likes to pay calls on former British colonies that are now independent republics, to remind them of their links with Britain. Such calls are not without their dangers, as Harold Macmillan saw when Elizabeth proposed to visit Ghana at a time of unrest and violence there. As Britain's prime minister at the time, Macmillan saw it as his duty to advise against the trip. Ghana, he told Elizabeth, was no fit place for a woman. "I am not going as a woman," Elizabeth informed him "I am going as the queen."

Even so, she could be in danger, Macmillan persisted. "Danger," retorted Elizabeth, "is part of the job."

*

Elizabeth's disregard for danger can cause problems for her security men. There have been many threats against her life over the years. One threat was received just as she was about to leave on a tour of rural England. She refused to cancel the tour. "It will be difficult to protect you in an area of narrow, winding roads and high hedges," she was told. "At least change the route, Ma'am." Again she refused. In the face of such royal obstinacy, all her security men could do, in addition to the customary precautions, was instruct her chauffeur to drive as fast as possible past any obvious danger points, such as crossroads. And even those instructions had to be given in secret for fear that Elizabeth would countermand them.

*

Only a month later came another threat. Elizabeth would be assassinated during her visit to York, threatened an anonymous letter writer. Despite the assassination of President Kennedy in Dallas not long before, Elizabeth again refused to cancel the visit or even vary her planned program, which included a stately drive through the city streets in an open, horse-drawn carriage. Unknown to her, her security men again took extra precautions. Troopers of the Household Cavalry, who escorted her on that drive through York, positioned themselves so that the jogging bodies of horses and riders formed a moving screen around her.

There was yet another threat that she would be blown up with a bomb when she opened Parliament. Again she insisted on going through with the traditional ceremony, though the Parliament buildings were searched from top to bottom ahead of her arrival and trained marksmen watched over her from adjoining rooftops as she rode through London's streets.

*

Ever since Guy Fawkes and his fellow conspirators tried to blow up king and Parliament with thirty-six barrels of gunpowder in 1605, it has been part of the British tradition to search chambers, passages, and vaults ahead of the annual opening ceremony. By the early part of Elizabeth's reign tradition had descended into mere stage acting, the search being carried out by Yeomen of the Guard in their colorful Tudor uniforms and equipped with nothing more formidable than old-fashioned pikes. But threats against Elizabeth's life coupled with assassinations around the world—President Kennedy in Dallas, President Sadat in Egypt, Elizabeth's uncle, Earl Mountbatten, in Ireland— mean that it is now carried out in earnest. The Yeomen of the Guard may still lend color to the scene, but the real work is done by police with sniffer dogs, soldiers equipped with sophisticated detection devices, and experts of London's bomb squad.

*

Elizabeth's uncle, Earl Mountbatten, had not yet been assassinated when she celebrated her silver jubilee (twenty- five years on the throne) in 1977. To celebrate, she planned to visit every part of Britain. Her security men advised against going to Northern Ireland because of the IRA. Again, Elizabeth declined to listen to them. "I was crowned Queen of the United Kingdom," she said. "That means Great Britain *and* Northern Ireland." And to Northern Ireland she went, taking Philip and Andrew, still a school- boy at the time, along with her.

She was equally determined, in 1984, to keep her promise to visit Jordan's King Hussein and his wife, Queen

Noor, the American-born daughter of Najeeb Halaby, former head of Pan American. Some of her advisers had not liked the idea from the start. Bordered as it is by Israel and Syria, Jordan is hardly the ideal vacation spot and Hussein hardly the most secure of monarchs, even if he has been fortunate enough to survive no fewer than fifteen attempts on his life. But Elizabeth, having accepted his invitation, was determined to go through with it. Not even a terrorist bombing campaign in Amman, the Jordanian capital, two days before her departure from London (one bomb exploded; two more were discovered in time and rendered harmless) could shake her resolve. The result was the most heavily guarded royal tour ever. A special flight plan was devised to avoid flying over Israel, Syria, or Lebanon. Her aircraft, for the first time, was fitted with American-made antimissile devices and flown by a pilot specially trained in missile evasion techniques. A squad of Britain's elite S.A.S. troops flew in disguise ahead of her to Jordan to help guard her when she got there. For Elizabeth's arrival, the airport at Amman was hemmed in by Hussein's handpicked Bedouin fighting men. Jeeps fitted with machine guns protected her car front and rear, with more machine guns set up at each intersection, as she was swept from airport to palace at a mile a minute; much to the disappointment of a bunch of British youngsters who had turned out to see her. Told later of the kids' disappointment, Elizabeth insisted on going to their school to see them.

*

Elizabeth's sense of royal duty, her refusal to be deterred by possible danger, has rubbed off on her children. "If someone is going to shoot you, there isn't much you can do about it," says Charles philosophically. "If you're going to worry about it, you might as well give up." And he, in turn, has infected Diana with the same philosophical attitude.

133

Visiting Edinburgh on her own not long after she married Charles, she refused to have any change made in her official schedule despite the fact that a letter bomb had been delivered at city hall just ahead of her arrival in protest against her visit.

Because they accept flowers and gifts from all and sundry in the course of their walkabouts, she and Charles are more vulnerable than most. Oblivious of possible danger—again a firebomb had gone off in protest ahead of their arrival—Diana accepted a string bag that was thrust at her during a walkabout in Wales and passed it to Charles. He peered suspiciously at the bag's contents—two round grayish white objects. "What are they?" he asked. In fact, they were nothing more lethal than turnips. "Not the exploding kind, I hope," quipped Charles when he found out.

*

Mystery still surrounds the slaying in Bermuda in 1973 of the island's governor, Sir Richard Sharples, and his aide, Captain Hugh Sayers. It happened just after the frigate *Minerva*, with Charles on board, had visited the island, and one theory is that the two men were killed because Sayers was mistaken for Charles. Certainly royal security men were not prepared to take any chances, and when the *Minerva* next called at Bermuda it was without Charles. He was temporarily transferred to the survey ship *Fox* ahead of the visit and transferred back after.

*

Princess Anne had an even closer call only four months after her wedding to Mark Philips. They were driving back to the palace from a charity function one night when they were held up by a gunman intent on kidnapping Anne. Their chauffeur was shot in the chest, their bodyguard in the shoulder. A journalist who intervened was also shot in the chest, and a policeman who sprinted across the road to the rescue was wounded in the stomach. The gunman wrenched open the car door and grabbed Anne by the wrist. Mark locked an arm around her waist to hold her back. "You've got to come with me," the gunman yelled at her. "I'll get a million for you." Throughout Anne herself remained not only icily calm, but regally polite. "*Please* go away," she told the would-be kidnapper. "Leave me alone and don't be so silly." She was finally saved by a burly Cockney, Ron Russell, who ran to her rescue, dodged a bullet, and felled her assailant with a punch. For saving her daughter, Elizabeth awarded Russell the George Cross, Britain's highest award for civilian bravery. A day later, despite her ordeal, Anne was again carrying out public engagements as usual. "It's no good sitting down and brooding about things," she said. However, she did take the extra precaution of arriving for this particular public engagement in a horse box instead of in one of the royal cars.

*

Anne is a tough and determined young woman and never more so than in working for her favorite charity, Britain's Save the Children Fund. Charity work, to Anne, is not simply a matter of donning her glad rags and attending money-raising functions, though she does that, too. Once a year she dons a bush hat, sleeveless shirt, and khaki skirt (or similar) and goes out into the field to see how the money she has helped to raise is being spent and what else is needed. Such treks take her to areas as harsh and hazardous as anything her father or brothers have visited. In 1982, for instance, she visited refugee camps in the war zone between Somalia and Ethiopia. Then, against the wishes of her security advisers, she insisted on going to war-torn Beirut, where she visited the American University Hospital to comfort children wounded in the fighting. The following

135

year found her in yet more refugee camps, this time on the Afghanistan–Pakistan border, where Afghanistan tribesmen told her that what they really needed were "more guns, Your Majesty." The next year, 1984, saw her in Gambia, in western Africa, where she personally hauled on the rope when her car had to be ferried across a river in order to reach a leper colony she had insisted on including in her schedule.

*

That burly Ron Russell, though unarmed, dashed to Anne's rescue despite the two guns the kidnapper was pointing at him was in keeping with the fiercely loyal affection most British have for the royal family. Nothing provokes the average Briton more than a display of disloyalty toward Elizabeth or any of her family. The former Lord Altrincham (who later resigned his title to become plain John Grigg) was publicly slapped across the face by an irate loyalist for writing an article in which he likened Elizabeth to "a priggish schoolgirl." Elizabeth's Scottish subjects were particularly up in arms. The Earl of Strathmore wanted "the bounder" shot, while the Duke of Argyll thought shooting too good. He suggested that the article writer should be hanged, drawn and quartered in the old tradition. An article in America's *Saturday Evening Post* by Malcolm Muggeridge, formerly editor of *Punch*, aroused similar fury in Britain. For describing Elizabeth as "dowdy, frumpy, and banal" Muggeridge was spat upon in the street and found his contract with a leading Sunday newspaper abruptly terminated. A left-wing councilor who pointedly omitted to rise to his feet when a toast to Elizabeth was proposed had his wineglass snatched and the contents poured over his head. A freelance journalist hawking phoney transcripts of alleged telephone calls between Diana in London and Charles in Australia ended up with his car window smashed and the tires slashed, while a shopkeeper who thought to attract more business by displaying a nude mock-up of Diana—her face superimposed on another girl's body—succeeded only in having a brick heaved through his window.

*

Gifts from loyal subjects in Britain and elsewhere, and even from people who owe Elizabeth II no allegiance, arrive constantly at Buckingham Palace. William's and Henry's births saw the palace inundated with baby clothes of every kind. An entire crèche of babies could not have worn them all, and most were passed on by Diana and Charles to children's hospitals and charities. Among the largest gifts ever to be manhandled through the palace gates was a native war canoe measuring twenty-seven feet from stem to stern. The smallest consisted of four grains of rice. Viewed under a magnifying glass, each grain was found to have a minute landscape painted on it. With food rationing still in force in Britain when Elizabeth and Philip were married in 1947, Americans took pity on them and showered them with a staggering 32,000 food parcels. Another gift from America later, from Texas, was a bale of cotton. Normally a letter of thanks for such gifts is deemed sufficient acknowledgement by Elizabeth. But this time she decided to send a portrait of herself as a reciprocal gift. Delighted by this royal response, the mayor of Edinburgh, Texas, convened a public meeting so that the whole town could see the queen's gift opened. Delight turned to disappointment when the crate was opened and found to contain only packing materials. Someone at Buckingham Palace had omitted to include the actual portrait. Of course, the mistake was rectified as soon as Elizabeth heard what had happened.

Palace Secrets

Small girls who get to see Elizabeth II on her royal visits to various parts of Britain are sometimes so disappointed by her appearance that they burst into tears. Instead of the fairy-tale queen they had expected, they see only a short, middle-aged, motherly looking woman. "She isn't a real queen," they sob. "She isn't wearing a crown."

In fact, Elizabeth rarely wears a crown, though she has two. One she wears only once a year, and the other she will never wear again; it is used only for the actual crowning of each new monarch. Though it is still known as St. Edward's crown, this second crown is no longer the one originally worn by Edward the Martyr, the murdered Saxon boy-king after whom it is named. Oliver Cromwell, when he overthrew King Charles I and made himself dictator in the seventeenth century, had that one destroyed. So a new one had to be made when Charles II was brought back as king. It is on the large size for Elizabeth, having been fashioned in the days when kings wore periwigs; it is a weighty concoction of gold, diamonds, rubies, emeralds, sapphires, and pearls that turns the scale at five pounds.

Alone among Britain's monarchs—if royal legend can be believed—Elizabeth II has worn St. Edward's Crown not once, but twice. When it was placed on her head at her coronation was the second time. How this came about is a touching human story.

More than anyone, it was Elizabeth's grandmother, Queen Mary, who trained her to be a queen. More than anything, it was the old queen's wish to see her granddaughter crowned. But as Elizabeth's coronation drew near, her grandmother lay dying. She should not be disappointed, Elizabeth decided. So with the connivance of Winston Churchill, the crown was conveyed secretly one night from its vault in the Tower of London to Marlborough House, where Queen Mary lived. Elizabeth went there, too, and in the room where her grandmother lay dying, donned the great crown for her to see.

Queen Mary died soon after, shortly before Elizabeth's coronation. Normally, the death of someone so close to a king or queen would have seen the coronation postponed. But Queen Mary's dying wish was that the show should go on, and it did.

*

St. Edward's Crown will not be worn again until Charles is crowned King Charles III. The crown Elizabeth wears once a year, when she formally opens Parliament, is the Imperial State Crown. Slightly lighter than St. Edward's, it is still a formidable headgear. And valuable. Set into its gold base are five rubies, eleven emeralds, eighteen sapphires, 277 pearls, and a staggering 2,783 diamonds. One of the diamonds alone weighs 309 carats.

*

Even this lighter crown is difficult to wear, awkward to balance on the head. To accustom herself to wearing it afresh each year, Elizabeth has it taken to the palace a day or so ahead of the Parliament opening ceremony and gets in a spot of practice, wearing it as she sits at her desk doing her paperwork, as she nibbles on a cucumber sandwich at tea time, and as she bends and straightens to spoon dog food into the corgis' feeding bowls.

*

Riding sidesaddle is something else Elizabeth does only once a year, when she rides at the head of her guards for the annual June ceremony known as the Birthday Parade. While she rides a lot during her weekends at Windsor Castle, she normally sits astride. Riding sidesaddle is a different, more tricky technique that calls into play a different set of muscles. As with wearing the crown, Elizabeth likes to practice in advance, slipping away to the mews at the rear of her palace to get in a spot of sidesaddle riding in secret.

The horse she rides for her annual Birthday Parade is not one of her usual mounts but an animal specially trained by the Metropolitan Police so that it does not react to the sound of military bands or the frenzied cheering of the crowd. It did react, however, the year a youth in the forefront of the crowd whipped out a pistol, pointed it at Elizabeth, and fired a series of blanks. Expert horsewoman that she is, Elizabeth managed to control the horse as it reared and capered.

*

As well as riding sidesaddle, it is traditional that Elizabeth should appear at the Birthday Parade in a military tunic and hat and a long black skirt. Beneath the skirt, however, and unseen by the thousands of spectators lining the processional route, she also wears a pair of riding breeches to avoid chafing her legs.

It is also traditional that she arrive on the parade ground exactly as the clock strikes eleven in the morning, no easy task when the parade ground is half a mile from Buckingham Palace and she has to make the trip on horseback. Yet she is never late, thanks to a man who carefully conceals himself in the clock tower prior to her arrival. It is his job to advance or retard the mechanism so that the clock strikes the hour to coincide with Elizabeth's appearance on the parade ground.

*

Britain's Parliament, like the Congress of the United States, is divided into two chambers. While Washington has the Senate and the House of Representatives, London has its House of Lords and House of Commons. The real law-making body in Britain is the House of Commons—the House of Lords can only amend or delay any new law—and no king or queen has been allowed to enter the precincts of the Commons since King Charles II swooped down on it with his guards in 1602 and arrested some of the members. So Elizabeth, when she opens each new Parliament, can enter only the House of Lords. From there she sends a royal aide with the curious title of Black Rod to summon members of the House of Commons to hear her speech detailing how Britain will be run for the next year.

It is indicative of what little real power the queen actually has that the speech she makes is not hers at all. It is written for her by the prime minister, and she must read it word for word as written.

*

The business of Black Rod is another traditional slice of ceremonial playacting. To demonstrate that they are not merely royal lackeys, members of the House of Commons always station a lookout man to tell them when the queen's messenger is coming. At the warning shout of "Black Rod," they slam the door of the chamber in his face. To gain admission and deliver Elizabeth's summons to attend upon her, he must then rap three times on the door with his staff of office.

Another piece of traditional playacting involves a member of the House of Commons who sees nothing of all this. He has his own special part to play elsewhere. Before Elizabeth leaves for Parliament, he presents himself at Buckingham Palace, surrenders himself to her, and is then "held hostage" there as a guarantee of her safe return.

*

While no king or queen since Charles I has ever been allowed officially to enter the House of Commons, Elizabeth in fact has done so. During World War II the chamber was wrecked by German bombs and rebuilt afterward. Elizabeth's father, King George VI, said he would very much like to see what the new chamber looked like. As it was not yet in use, it was decided that the safety of members would not be imperiled by permitting the king to look around, and he did so, taking his daughter with him.

*

As in everything else, Elizabeth is a perfectionist when it comes to tradition. Before her coronation, she not only had her crown taken to the palace so that she could accustom herself to wearing it, but was also concerned as to how she would manage the long trailing velvet robe she was also required to wear for part of the ceremony. That, she decided, would require practice, too. To avoid soiling the actual robe, she paraded around her palace wearing one of the long, heavy damask tablecloths normally used for royal banquets.

The coronation ceremony is a complex ritual that takes some four and a half hours to run its course. To ensure that nothing went wrong, there were several rehearsals ahead of time. One of these had reached the point where Philip was called upon to kneel in front of his wife and swear allegiance to her. Macho as he is, young and high-spirited as he was at the time, Philip was inclined to treat the business of oath taking, kissing Elizabeth, and touching the crown on her head as a joke. To Elizabeth, it was no joking matter and, as Philip made to walk away, she was quick to summon him back and insist that he do it again.

*

As part of her actual coronation ceremony, Elizabeth was briefly screened from view while she divested herself of her robe and jewels so that her hands, brow, and head could be anointed with holy oil. The oil is made from a secret formula, and there was consternation just ahead of the coronation when it was discovered that the pharmacy that had been making it since Queen Victoria's day had gone out of business. Royal aides succeeded in tracking down an elderly member of the pharmacy family, but she did not have the formula. Nor did she know who did. But she did have a few drops of oil leftover from the coronation of Elizabeth's father that she had kept as a souvenir. The leftover drops were passed to a London chemist who loyally gave up smoking to improve his sense of smell while analyzing the drops and preparing a fresh batch of oil.

*

Readers who think that anointing the brow and breast with oil is a bit quaint should take note of what happened at the coronation of King Birendra of Nepal, which Prince Charles attended in 1975. Instead of being simply dabbed with holy oil, King Birendra was smeared with holy mud concocted from dirt collected from a Himalayan peak, the bed of a lake, an anthill, and the doorstep of a prostitute's house.

*

Following her coronation, Elizabeth rode through London in the four-ton gold coach built originally for the coronation of George IV. The coach is unusual in that it has no coachman. Elizabeth's great-grandfather, King Edward VII, had the coachman's box removed so that people could see him better. That Elizabeth was seen more clearly still was due to the fact that, for her coronation, the coach was fitted with concealed lighting operated from batteries tucked away under the seats. Magnificent though the coach looks, it is not the most comfortable form of transport. To ensure Elizabeth of the best possible ride, its early-nineteenth-century wheels were shod afresh with twentieth-century rubber tires. A couple of labor-saving devices were also secretly installed.

As she rode through the streets of London after her coronation, Elizabeth not only wore her crown but appeared to be holding two other symbols of queenship, a scepter and a gold ball known as the orb. In fact, she was not. The weight of the orb was actually taken by a concealed shelf, while the scepter was held at the correct angle by a hidden bracket.

*

Thanks largely to Elizabeth's insistence on perfection, her coronation ceremony, long and complex though it was, passed off without a hitch. Not so her father's. King George VI was unable to read his oath of kingship properly, though not because of his stammer. The archbishop had his thumb stuck over some of the wording. The Lord Chamberlain got into a muddle while trying to belt on the king's sword, and George had to take over and do it himself. The archbishop nearly placed the crown on his head the wrong way round. "You've got it back to front," hissed the king. Finally, when it was time for the king to stand in all his crowned glory, he stumbled and nearly fell because one of the dignitaries around him was standing on the royal robe.

*

Despite this series of minor mishaps, the coronation of Elizabeth's father was still an improvement on past ceremonies. History records that one of England's early Saxon kings, Edwy, disappeared in the middle of his coronation. Archbishop Dunstan went in search of him and found him making love to his teenage wife on the floor of the next chamber. William the Conqueror's coronation ended in a brawl between William's Norman bodyguards and the native Saxons. Several people were killed and the coronation venue, Westminster Abbey, set on fire. The first Elizabeth, regarded by the Church as "a bastard and a heretic," had difficulty finding a churchman willing to crown her. Charles II's coronation had to be postponed while a new crown was made to replace the one destroyed by Oliver Cromwell. Queen Anne was so fat and gout-ridden that she could not stand at her coronation and the ceremony of buckling on the royal spurs had to be abandoned because the straps would not go round her swollen ankles. That part of the coronation ceremony has never been revived. George IV, for his coronation, surrounded himself with a bodyguard of prizefighters disguised as royal pages to prevent his discarded wife, Queen Caroline, from barging into the ceremony and insisting on being crowned with him. When Queen Victoria was crowned, the archbishop forced the massive coronation ring onto the wrong finger. And there it stuck. Victoria had to go to bed that night with the huge ring still on her finger, and it was not until the following morning that the diligent application of soap enabled her to free herself of it.

*

Prince Charles' investiture as Prince of Wales at Caernarvon Castle in 1969 was like a minicoronation. Lacking a crown, he decided to have a special coronet made for the occasion. To ensure that it would fit rather better than his mother's crown does, he telephoned the firm that makes his father's hats and asked if he could borrow their gadget for measuring heads. Certainly, they said. "But it takes and expert to handle it." So they sent their expert along to the palace with it. It was as well they did so. The head-measuring gadget proved to be an ingenious assembly of rods and springs that resembles nothing so much as a medieval instrument of torture.

*

Perfectionist that she is, Elizabeth prides herself that her royal banquets (such as the one she gave at Windsor Castle for President and Mrs. Reagan) always run like clockwork, with everyone served at the same time and dirty dishes all cleared at the same time—no easy task when there are several hundred guests sitting down to dinner. The secret of why everything runs so smoothly is hidden among the flower arrangements that adorn the banquet hall. Sets of miniature traffic lights, operated by the royal steward, change from color to color in a code that instructs royal pages and footmen when to do what.

*

There was something of a panic at the palace one night when the servant whose duty it is to check that the royal gold is still all there after a banquet reported that a gold dish used to serve ice cream was missing. Despite an intensive search, it was nowhere to be found. Next morning an embarrassed footman turned up at the gold pantry, dish in hand. There had been some ice cream left on it, he explained, and he had taken it to his room as a late-night snack. There was another occasion when a gold fork was missing after a banquet. That too was found eventually. It had fallen into one of the garbage bins in which wasted food is dumped to be taken to Windsor and fed to the pigs on the royal farm there.

*

Because they were hosted at Windsor Castle, President and Mrs. Reagan missed seeing one of Buckingham Palace's most novel secrets. Guests invited to royal banquets at the palace assemble first in what is known as the White Drawing Room while the royals ready themselves in the Royal Closet next door. Guests assembled and everything ready, Elizabeth presses a concealed button in the Royal Closet. To the surprise of guests in the White

Drawing Room, an entire china cabinet swings smoothly out of place in one corner of the room, revealing a doorway through which Elizabeth and accompanying members of her family can make a spectacular entrance.

*

Elsewhere in the palace, adorning one of the walls, is a painting that is not quite what it seems. It is a family group—Elizabeth, Philip, Charles, Anne, and one of the corgis—painted in the days when Charles and Anne were still small children. But just a moment. Are those really Elizabeth's legs? Or Philip's hands? No, they are not. Elizabeth commissioned the painting as a companion piece to a similar family group painted in her own childhood while she was still a princess. The painting was not yet finished when her father died and she found herself queen. With all the extra work she and Philip had to do in those early days of her monarchy, there was no time to pose further for the artist. So that the painting could be finished, a suitably tall footman was told to act as stand-in for Philip, while the loyal Bobo MacDonald served as a model for Elizabeth herself. In consequence, the Elizabeth in the painting has Bobo's legs, while Philip has been given the footman's hands.

*

Privileged guests invited to stay overnight at Buckingham Palace are sometimes surprised to find themselves with a dressing room that boasts no fewer than three washbasins, labeled respectively "Hands," "Face," and "Teeth." They were installed originally by Elizabeth's great-grandfather, King Edward VII, a man whose passion for cleanliness almost matched the enthusiasm with which he seduced other men's wives.

*

The palace also has its own small movie theater. What was once a dining room for royal servants has been fitted with a screen and tip-up seats upholstered in blue plush so that the royals and their friends can watch the latest movies in privacy and comfort. Elizabeth likes musicals, Charles and Philip both enjoy a good belly-laugh comedy, while Anne is partial to westerns. Aboard the royal yacht the dining room can also be used as a movie theater. A sliding panel goes back to reveal a movie screen, with projectors situated in the adjoining kitchen. At Balmoral Castle and Sandringham the ballroom also does duty as a movie theater, with a supply of the latest movies sent there from London, while at Windsor Castle movies are sometimes shown on a portable screen set up in one of the state rooms.

*

As President Eisenhower discovered when he was a guest there, Balmoral Castle, the family's Scottish retreat, is a throwback to Victorian times, and not only in its architecture. Inside too the ghost of Queen Victoria still lingers. The wallpaper still carries her *VR* cipher (for *Victoria Regina*), and everywhere are paintings by her favorite artist, Edwin Landseer. Meals in the dining room are eaten under the painted gaze of her many children, while carpet and curtains in the drawing room are patterned in the red-and-gray Balmoral tartan designed by her husband, Albert, Prince Consort.

*

"When in Scotland, do as the Scots" is the royal family's unofficial motto. So, once at Balmoral, they change quickly into kilts. They are awakened each morning by the sound of bagpipes—Elizabeth has her own piper—and entertained after dinner each evening by a contingent of four burly

149

pipers in full Highland dress, pipes going full blast as the musicians parade around the dining room.

If Balmoral Castle is Victorian in its decor, Windsor Castle is no less Edwardian in the lavishness of the hospitality Elizabeth dispenses there during that June week of horse racing and feminine fashion known as Royal Ascot. To be invited to Windsor Castle for Ascot week is to live briefly in the grand style of a vanished era. From the moment of arrival until the moment of departure, Elizabeth's guests hardly have to do a thing for themselves. Immediately upon arrival, their cars are whisked away to be washed and polished. Luggage likewise vanishes. When next seen, shoes have been polished, dresses pressed, shirts laundered, suits valeted, and everything arranged neatly in wardrobes and chests of drawers. Guests hardly have to dress themselves; there are maids and valets at hand to help them. They find their favorite drink automatically served to them before dinner (their taste has been ascertained in advance), and each morning a tea tray appears silently at each bedside along with a selection of the day's newspapers.

*

Elizabeth has several tricks of the trade to ease the strain of the public appearances she is constantly obliged to make. Traveling by train, she will sit at a window waving to the crowds. Out of sight below window level, she usually nudges her shoes off to ease her aching feet and sits with her feet up to rest her legs. Her wave is a special one, taught to her by her parents, designed to ease the strain on wrist and arm. For hand shaking she keeps her hand limp and the little finger well out of harm's way. She also wears gloves. It was Barbra Streisand who once asked her why she always kept her gloves on when shaking hands. The question took

Elizabeth so aback that she could only murmur in reply that she didn't really know. In fact, the gloves are a protection against scratches from other people's rings and fingernails.

Elizabeth's Rolls-Royce has a special armrest set at just the right height to support her arm while she waves at crowds. Built specially for her at a cost of $90,000 as a gift to mark her 1977 silver jubilee, the car also has a raised seat and a transparent rear roof so that she can be clearly seen. The wide central armrest conceals a radio, cassette player (she likes to listen to military bands while traveling), and a dictating machine as well as a small compartment in which she stores the canister of barley sugar that travels with her wherever she goes. Sucking a piece of barley sugar from time to time relieves tension, she finds.

*

Unlike her daughter-in-law Diana, Elizabeth is not good at small talk (as her reply to Barbra Streisand reveals) and has sometimes been known to dry up completely in the course of a royal walkabout. Indeed, it was quite common for her to do so when she was younger. Philip would dash to her rescue, bridging any awkward gap in conversation with a witty remark. "Buck up, sweetie," he would whisper encouragingly to Elizabeth.

*

Diana, on the other hand, is inclined to chat away so much that Charles has sometimes to usher her along if they are not to be too late for their next engagement. William and Henry, as they grow up, may have cause to regret that their mother is such a chatterbox. Charles may not mind such wifely revelations as the fact that he sometimes does the washing up, but William, in schooldays, may not like being teased about whether he still dribbles or spits, as Diana has revealed he did in babyhood.

Unlike her royal mother-in-law, Diana does not wear

gloves for protection. Nor does she copy Elizabeth's rather limp handshake. Her handshake is "a real one, not like a dead fish," according to a blind woman with whom she paused to chat when she and Charles were in New Zealand. The fact that she does not wear gloves coupled with the hundreds of handshakes she may be forced to endure in the course of a day sometimes means that, come evening, her hands are sore. She copies her husband's secret remedy for tender hands and gives them a long soak in cold water.

There was concern among her royal in-laws, when she first married Charles, that Diana might not stand up to the rigors of the royal round. Such fears were not helped by a polo game she attended a week before the wedding. Premarriage tension caused her to burst into tears as a score of cameras were pointed at her and flee the ground. However, her in-laws' fears have proved groundless. The way she has handled things since marriage has quickly made her the new superstar of the royal road show. Though she concealed the fact well, at first—on her own admission—she found it difficult to cope with the pressures of royal life. "I have learned a lot during the past three or four months," she revealed during the couple's 1983 tour of Canada, "and feel that I am doing my job better now."

*

Diana's occasional failure has not necessarily been her fault. It was not her fault that her first ship launching did not go off entirely as planned. Twice she whacked the bow of the vessel with the traditional bottle of champagne, and twice the bottle remained unbroken. "I don't think it will ever break," she sighed. But Charles lent a helping hand and, between them, it did.

*

Elizabeth's grandfather, King George V, gave sound advice to his eldest son, who later became Duke of

Windsor, on how best to cope with a busy round of public engagements. "Never refuse an invitation to take the weight off your feet," he told him, "and never miss an opportunity to relieve yourself. You never know when the chance may come again."

*

Philip does not wait for an invitation to take the weight off his feet. The secret of his ability to put in an eighteen-hour day, as he often does, lies in the fact that any gap between functions finds him looking around for the nearest available bed or couch. He lies down, stretches out, and catnaps. Like Winston Churchill, he has the knack of waking when he wants without the need for an alarm clock.

*

People meeting Philip in the course of his worldwide travels are often surprised at how much he knows about them. Said the mayor of San Francisco, after Philip visited the city some years ago: "He knew all about me. He even knew I was born in Greece." The secret of Philip's seemingly vast knowledge is a microfilm index of people, places, and things of over 70,000 references, constantly updated. A quick check of this system also helps him not to make the same speech twice in the same place.

Though his aides may do much of the research for him, Philip (unlike Elizabeth) is his own speech writer. When he is making what he regards as an important speech, he even rehearses it in advance, standing at a reading desk in his study and declaiming aloud to an empty room. Before starting, he switches on a tape recorder. Listening to the playback enables him to judge exactly how the speech comes over.

*

It is largely thanks to Philip that Elizabeth is now better at delivering speeches than she used to be. For years she affected a style of enunciation that one critic labeled bluntly as "a pain in the neck." The comment stung. Philip suggested she use his tape recorder trick of listening to herself to change the way she spoke. She did, and it worked.

*

It was Philip too who, unseen, turned Elizabeth's first-ever telecast into such a spectacular success. Elizabeth was nervous of appearing on television and rejected several approaches from the BBC. But sooner or later, she knew, she had to take the plunge. She decided to do so during a visit to Canada but was so nervous that her first rehearsal was little short of a disaster. Nevertheless, she was determined to go ahead. She had another rehearsal immediately before the actual telecast, which was to be live. She nudged her shoes off under the table in an attempt to relax more, but she still looked absolutely terrified and stumbled through her script. Philip, watching her on a monitor, had a bright idea. "Please give the queen a message from me," he said to the studio manager. "Tell her to remember the wailing and gnashing of teeth." Puzzled, the studio manager passed on the cryptic message. If he did not know what it meant, Elizabeth did. It was a line Philip had missed out when reading the lesson at a church service in Ottawa, and she had been teasing him about it since. She gave a glowing smile—at the exact moment the transmission went live—and the image of a happy, smiling queen marked her first television appearance.

*

If it was Philip who saved Elizabeth on that occasion, it was a humble footman who came to her rescue on another. She was about to leave for an important public function when she was seized by a sudden and persistent attack of hiccups. Various traditional cures were quickly tried—

hands were clapped loudly behind her, a door was slammed suddenly with a bang—but failed to work. It began to look as if she might have to call off her engagement. Queen Elizabeth II could not possibly appear in public hiccuping uncontrollably. Then a footman suggested trying a cure he had learned from his grandmother. "Fill a glass with water," he explained "and then drink it from the wrong side, holding the glass in such a way that you can seal your ears with your thumbs while drinking." It sounded rather like turning into a contortionist, but Elizabeth decided to give it a go and retreated into a bathroom to do so. When she emerged again a few minutes later, she was all smiles, the hiccups gone. "It worked," she proclaimed triumphantly.

The Royal Road Show

Elizabeth II is the most-traveled monarch in Britain's history and arguably the world's most traveled woman. Her 1983 visit to President Reagan in California brought her globe-trotting to a total of three-quarters of a million miles, and she has been to a score of other countries since. Prince Philip, because he travels around on his own as well as accompanying Elizabeth wherever she goes, has traveled twice, perhaps three times, as far. He reckons to average 75,000 miles a year. Charles and Diana cannot yet match such mileages. But they have time ahead of them and will almost certainly outstrip Charles' parents in the years to come, while the future King William V, their baby son, seems destined to surpass both his parents and grandparents. He made an early start. He was little more than nine months old when his parents took him with them to Australia in 1983, the youngest member of the family ever to undertake a royal tour.

*

For Diana, as well as William, that trip to Australia constituted her first-ever overseas tour, though not her first overseas engagement as a member of the royal family. On her honeymoon, she hosted Egypt's President Sadat and his wife aboard the royal yacht and not long after flew from

157

Britain to Monaco to represent her royal mother-in-law at the funeral of Princess Grace.

*

Diana is without doubt the new megastar of the royal road show. In Melbourne, Australia, nearly a quarter of a million people packed the city center the day Diana and Charles were there. In the face of such Diana worship, Australia's Labor government found itself obliged to postpone its idea of turning the country from a monarchy into a republic. "If it went to a vote, then it's clear that the people of Australia just wouldn't have it," said a former prime minister, Sir William McMahon.

In all the frenzied, hysterical scenes that have erupted around Diana, notably in Australia and Canada, only once has her nerve failed her. That was in Brisbane, Australia, where a mob of a hundred thousand people broke through the barricades and surged around the royal couple, momentarily cutting her off from Charles. He struggled his way back to her side, pushing and pulling her through the mob while police joined hands to form a protective circle and tried to clear the way ahead. The experience so shook Diana that a doctor was summoned. But ten minutes' rest and a long, cold drink saw her back to normal, sufficiently recovered from her ordeal to appear again in public, though this time safely esconced on the town-hall balcony.

*

Before each royal tour Diana always settles down to do a spot of homework. Before visiting Wales, for instance, she learned enough Welsh to thank people for flowers and gifts and even to make a brief formal speech in the language. Before touring Australia she learned that country's national anthem by heart, while Charles, prior to their visit to New Zealand, learned enough to make a speech to the country's Maoris in their own tongue.

Equally, Charles spoke the local pidgin when opening the new Parliament building in Papua New Guinea. "Dispela emi bigpela haus bilong of Man Meri bilong Papua New Guinea." Translated, his words meant: "This big house belongs to all the people of Papua New Guinea."

*

Elizabeth's first-ever tour as queen still ranks as her longest. It took her around the world and lasted six months. During that time she toured ten countries and journeyed a total of 50,000 miles—18,850 by sea, 19,650 by air, 9,900 by road, and 1,600 by train.

*

Philip once managed to visit twenty-five different countries over a period of six months. And on the tour of South America, over the course of forty-four days he managed to sandwich in fifty receptions, thirty-four official dinners and luncheons, sixty-eight visits to factories, plantations, churches, and schools, and thirty speeches.

*

Credit for hauling royal tours out of the horse-and-buggy age and into the twentieth century goes to Philip. He pointed the way even before Elizabeth became queen. As a princess, she and Philip were due to visit Canada as deputies for her desperately ill father. As with previous royal tours, they were to have gone there by sea. Then the condition of Elizabeth's father worsened, and he had to undergo further surgery. She refused to leave Britain until she knew he was safely over the operation. By then it was too late to reach Canada on time, and it seemed that the tour schedule, which had taken six months to arrange, would be thrown completely out of gear.

"We can still make it on time if we fly," said Philip.

Britain's government was horrified. Far too risky, said

the prime minister. But Philip argued his case and won the day. The flight, in those prejet days of 1951, took seventeen hours.

*

It was Philip, too, who first took the royal road show to places previously thought inaccessible. Bored with palace life, missing the old days of seagoing adventure, Philip took off in the royal yacht in 1956 on the most adventurous royal tour ever. He was away four months and journeyed 39,000 miles, visiting places no member of the royal family had ever been—the uranium mines in Australia's Rum Jungle, hydroelectric plants in the Snowy Mountains, the Falkland Islands, Deception Island, Tristan da Cunha, and the Antarctic. He used a canvas-skinned longboat, which he helmed himself, to get ashore on Tristan da Cunha, and when he spotted a whaler one day, nothing would satisfy him but that he must be slung from royal yacht to whaler in a wicker basket. "He stunk to high heaven when he got back," one of the yacht's crew recalls. Philip's sons have done much to emulate him since—Charles has ventured into the Canadian Arctic and Andrew has been even further north, to Cape Columbia, the place where the American explorer Admiral Robert Peary set out to become the first man to reach the pole—but Philip's 1956 Antarctic expedition still rates as the most adventurous.

*

Elizabeth's regal globetrotting has brought her many unusual experiences. She has watched sheep shearing in Australia's Outback, lumberjacking in Canada, and weird fertility rites on the island of New Britain. She has been serenaded by Maori chanting, conch shells, nose flutes, and cowhorn trumpets. She has watched native dancers perform in postage-stamp loincloths and bras fashioned from coconut shells. She has eaten from plates made from banana leaves, with her fingers (in Fiji) and with chopsticks (in Singapore). She found that she couldn't manage the chopsticks and resorted to a spoon. She has been fed such exotic delicacies as coral worms, roast bat, suckling pig, raw fish, shark-fin soup, barbecued turtle, and breadfruit. In the Seychelles she ate coco-de-mer, which is said to be the fruit with which Eve tempted Adam in the Garden of Eden. And each fresh trip to Fiji—she has been there several times as the island's queen—means downing a drink of the local firewater. Called *kava*, it is a liquor so fiery it numbs the mouth. It also tastes like soap. But Elizabeth knocks it back without flinching. Only one drink has ever brought a change of expression to her royal features—a cup of frothy green tea she was served in Japan. She grimaced as she drank it but said only that she found the flavor "rather surprising."

*

Elizabeth's country home at Sandringham bulges like a museum with all her travel souvenirs—spears, boomerangs, ornamental daggers, fans, turbans, shawls, and fly whisks, native furniture and clothing, whale teeth and shark teeth, elephant tusks, lion skins and leopard skins, Indian headdresses, and drinking cups made of horn. She has, among other things, a cloak made of kiwi feathers, a bedspread fashioned from tree bark, a tortoise egg over one hundred years old, a paperweight made from a tiger's paw, and another from the fossilized bone of a dinosaur.

But royal aides drew the line at one travel souvenir she was offered. A sultan had brought along two cheetah cubs he wanted to give her. It would amuse her to play with them, he said.

"But won't they bite her?" asked her aides.

"Oh, no," said the sultan. "At least, not until they are

old enough to be fed on raw meat."

In the event, Elizabeth decided to stick to corgis.

*

Elizabeth is generally credited with pioneering the informal walkabouts that are now an integral part of the royal road show. She did her first in New Zealand in 1970. But her mother, in fact, did one long before that—in America in 1939. She was in New York with Elizabeth's father when, to everyone's surprise, she suddenly bobbed under the joined hands of their police cordon to mingle and chat with delighted New Yorkers.

*

Philip indulged in an unofficial walkabout of a rather different kind when he and Elizabeth visited New York in 1957. Having been shown around the Institute of Physics, he decided to take an incognito stroll through the city streets. So off he set along Lexington Avenue. He took a look at Forty-Second Street and Grand Central Station, emerging from the station by the Park Avenue exit. From there he walked to the Waldorf-Astoria, where he and Elizabeth were staying. There was a crowd outside the front of the hotel hoping to glimpse the royal couple, and Philip decided it would be easier to slip in through a side door. But he found a crowd gathered there, too. He shouldered his way through it—only to find the entrance to the hotel guarded by a burly New York cop. Failing to recognize the prince immediately, the cop barred the way. "It's all right— it's me," Philip said, grinning, and slipped past the cop into the hotel.

*

It was not the first time Elizabeth and Philip had been to the United States. They were there previously in 1951. Elizabeth was still a princess at the time, and President Truman took her along to meet his aging mother. Back in

Britain, shortly before, there had been a general election that had seen Winston Churchill again returned as prime minister. "I am so glad your father has been reelected," the president's mother congratulated King George VI's daughter.

*

Even in 1951 Elizabeth and Philip were by no means the first members of the royal family to visit the United States. Elizabeth's parents were there in 1939, and her great-grandfather, King Edward VII, as far back as 1860. He was still Prince of Wales at the time, young and unmarried, a most eligible bachelor, and so many young ladies and their hopeful parents crowded into New York's Academy of Music for a ball in his honor that the floor collapsed under the strain. A three-hour delay followed while workmen repaired the floor. Finally the dancing started again. But hardly had it done so than the band found itself competing with loud banging from beneath the floor. In the rush to complete the repair work one of the workmen had been nailed down under the new floorboards.

*

Prince Charles first visited the United States in 1970 when he was twenty-one. David Eisenhower took him to see the Washington Monument. Having sampled the view from the top, Charles suddenly suggested, "Let's run down the stairs." Suiting action to words, he raced at top speed down the 555 steps with David Eisenhower in hot pursuit and Secret Service agents assigned to guard the prince huffing and puffing a long way behind.

*

Andrew was seventeen when he carried out his first royal tour. The country selected was Canada, where he had been at school a year before. Main object of the tour was to be in Vancouver on Canada Day. But Andrew also undertook an

163

adventurous two-week canoe trek along the Coppermine River, living on a diet of dehydrated food and fish from the river, along with visits to Calgary (for the Stampede) and Cape Columbia, Canada's most northerly tip. While in the province of British Columbia he also visited the Pearson College of the Pacific. A Toronto public relations man, Jim McPhee, was assigned the task of preceding Andrew to check on arrangements for the visit. Arriving at what he took to be the college gates, he explained why he was there.

"Prince Andrew?" came the astonished reply. "You mean he's actually coming here? To visit us?"

What McPhee had taken for the college turned out to be a medium-security prison.

*

Philip, when he travels to other countries, has to have a passport just like everyone else. Elizabeth does not. As, theoretically, it is she who authorizes the issue of passports in Britain, it would be ridiculous for her to issue one to herself.

But she is still not free to go where she likes. Her foreign travels must accord with Britain's foreign policy. So it was not until fifteen years after the end of World War II that she was permitted to visit Germany, though her in-laws, Philip's sisters, lived there. She once went to South Africa as a princess but has not been back since becoming queen. Nor is she likely to in the foreseeable future. And she has never been to Russia, though there have been occasional overtures from the Soviets. But she has been to the United States five times, in 1951, 1957 (when she addressed the United Nations), 1959, 1976, and 1983, plus a brief stopover in Hawaii while on her way to Australia in 1970 and a private holiday divided between Kentucky and Wyoming in 1984.

*

Depending on its duration, it can take anything from six to eighteen months even to plan a royal tour. Planning starts with a large-scale map of the country or countries it is intended to visit. The map is spread out on the carpeted floor of Elizabeth's sitting room, with Elizabeth, Philip, and their aides crawling around on their hands and knees as they work out the itinerary. Colored tapes—red for air, blue for sea, green for train, and black for car—are superimposed on the map to show the intended route, with coloured pins literally pinpointing the various stopping places. That done, a three-man team of royal aides sets out to travel the route and report back. The team includes a detective to check on security arrangements, the Master of the Household—Elizabeth's majordomo—who ensures that sleeping and eating arrangements are satisfactory, and one of Elizabeth's private secretaries, busy throughout with a stopwatch. Every section of the journey, every stop, every reception, lunch, and banquet is timed to the minute. Elizabeth herself is sometimes amused by the exactness of her final schedule, though she realizes the necessity for fixed timing and would be the first to become impatient over any delay along the way. For a single luncheon during a tour of New Zealand her schedule detailed the time she should arrive, how long could be spent on prelunch drinks, what time she would sit down to eat, what time she must finish eating, and how long she could spend saying good-bye on her way out. Looking through the schedule, she noticed that this last item, saying good-bye, had been timed at seventeen minutes precisely. "I hope I don't spill my coffee," she joked. "There might not be time for a second cup."

Not that the planners always know best or necessarily get their own way. The first time she was to visit Washington, DC, for instance, Elizabeth was quick to realize that it would be night when she arrived there. "People won't be able to see me in the dark," she observed. In consequence, the planned schedule was rearranged to permit a daytime arrival in the American capital.

*

While Elizabeth flies to most places these days, a tour of any duration usually finds her magnificent royal yacht *Britannia* leaving Britain ahead of her to serve as a floating hotel when she gets to wherever she is going. Nearly half as long as the liner *Queen Elizabeth 2*, *Britannia* is as little like any ordinary yacht as Buckingham Palace is like an ordinary house. It's more a seagoing stately home. Folding doors enable its two main rooms to become a single handsome reception hall in which two hundred guests can be hosted without crowding. The dining table was originally designed to seat thirty-two people. Philip, when the yacht was first built, thought this hardly enough and took a party of royal aides and palace servants aboard to test things out. The result was the construction of two extensions to the dining table that now enable up to fifty-six people to sit down to dinner at one time.

*

Elizabeth and Philip each have a private sitting room aboard the yacht. An elevator links their sitting rooms with their sleeping quarters. Privacy in their sleeping quarters is ensured by the fact that the distance between the floor and portholes is two feet higher than normal, so no one on deck can peep in. Peace and quiet are ensured by having the crew of the yacht pad around in rubber-soled sneakers. And there are no shouted words of command when the royals are aboard. Instead, orders to the crew are given by means of colored signaling bats.

*

These days, the yacht is fitted with stabilizers. They were installed after a trip across the North Sea in weather so rough that Elizabeth was obliged to eat dinner with one hand while holding her plate in place with the other. Worse was to follow. She was awakened in the middle of the night by a loud crash. Switching on her lamp, she saw that her dressing table had broken free from its restraining hooks and was careening wildly about the cabin as the yacht rolled and rocked in the storm. Her hairbrushes and scent bottles had been thrown all over the cabin. Donning her robe, she summoned crewmen to manhandle the dressing table back into place and secure it with ropes. To her relief, her silver-backed hand mirror and cut-glass scent bottles were unbroken, though Philip was less fortunate with his collection of records. Many were broken, as was a lot of china and glass elsewhere aboard the yacht.

*

Elizabeth always travels in grand style. Not for her any question of crushing clothes into a couple of suitcases. Her coats and dresses are hung in two specially made portable wardrobes that are mounted on wheels to make for ease of handling. Gloves, handkerchiefs, lingerie, and the like are neatly layered in a matching chest of drawers. Half a dozen large trunks hold other items. Elaborately designed gowns for state banquets or balls each have a trunk to themselves. There are boxes for some three dozen hats, depending on the length of time she will be away, and more boxes for perhaps twice as many pairs of shoes. She seldom, if ever, wears all the shoes she takes along, though perhaps half a dozen pairs will be well-worn by the time she gets back. Royal travels are hard on the feet, so shoes she finds really comfortable are worn time and time again. With two exceptions, all her luggage is covered in matching blue leather. One of the exceptions is a crocodile dressing case that holds her thirty-piece set of silver brushes, combs, hand mirrors, and cosmetic containers. The other exception is a long, slender case of unique design. Custom-made to hold a selection of umbrellas and parasols, it was willed to her by her grandmother, Queen Mary.

*

In addition to clothes, Elizabeth takes along with her on her travels:

- two feather-filled pillows
- a hot-water bottle
- her own bath salts and pine-scented soap
- her own kid-covered lavatory seat
- a canister of her favorite China tea
- crates and crates of bottled water
- a supply of barley sugar
- two cameras—one movie, one still
- a selection of crossword puzzles
- a supply of black-edged notepaper

*

Having her own pillows along ensures her of a good night's rest. The hot-water bottle is a comfort if nights are chilly. The bottled water is a precaution against tummy upsets. The barley sugar is to suck if she feels tense or travel sick. A pot of her favorite tea, freshly brewed, serves as a stimulant, while tackling the crossword puzzles helps her to relax between engagements.

*

Philip has his own luggage along, of course. So do the couple's aides. They are usually accompanied by an entourage of thirty or more. These include:

- two ladies-in-waiting
- an equerry (male equivalent of a lady-in-waiting)
- a private secretary (maybe two)
- a press officer
- a physician

- Elizabeth's hairdresser
- two dressers (who look after Elizabeth's clothes)
- two valets (who do the same for Philip)
- two, perhaps three, stenographers
- a page
- one or two footmen
- maids (to look after the ladies-in-waiting)
- security men

*

The amount of luggage Elizabeth and Philip take with them when they travel came as a considerable shock to a New Zealand couple named Coles. They offered the hospitality of their country home to the couple for a relaxing weekend. Royal aides, it was suggested, could be accommodated in nearby cottages. The couple were naturally delighted when Elizabeth and Philip accepted their offer, but they were horrified when the royal luggage arrived on their doorstep. There was so much that it took two army trucks to transport it. "Where on earth are we going to put it all?" wailed poor Mrs. Coles. The problem was eventually resolved by stacking the whole lot in the billiard room—which effectively killed Mr. Coles' idea that he and Philip might have a game or two of billiards together during the weekend.

*

Dressers, valets, pages, and footmen work the longest hours when the royal road show goes on tour. It is their job to reach each overnight stopping place ahead of the royals and have everything unpacked and ready for their arrival, then pack again as soon as they have left next morning and race them to the next stopping place. Everything must be immediately at hand if Elizabeth is to keep to her tightly packed, intricately timed schedule. So her dressing table at each stopping place is set out exacty as the one back home in Buckingham Palace, hair brushes to her right, clothes brushes on her left, hand mirror and cosmetics directly ahead. Whatever desk she is using temporarily is similarly set out like her own desk at the palace, blotting pad front center, notepaper in a rack behind, dispatch box and pencils to her right, scribbling pad on her left. The clothes she will be wearing for her next public engagement must be pressed and laid out, together with jewelry, so that she can change with a minimum of delay.

Before leaving for a public function Elizabeth always likes to inspect herself from top to toe in a full-length mirror. The suite she was allotted in one small hotel did not possess one, however, and her servants promptly set about scouring the whole hotel for one. There was a long mirror fixed to one wall of the ladies' powder room, Elizabeth's dresser reported back. Her page and footmen thereupon unscrewed the mirror from the wall of the powder room and manhandled it to the royal suite, where they propped it in position with the aid of a stack of heavy books.

*

One thing Elizabeth does not take with her on her overseas travels is her crown. Neither of her two crowns nor their accompanying crown jewels may be taken out of Britain.

Nevertheless, Elizabeth takes a considerable collection of jewelry with her wherever she goes—tiaras, bracelets, necklaces, brooches, earrings, a shimmering mass of diamonds, rubies, pearls, sapphires, and amethysts. These are her own property, part of a fabulous personal collection of jewels she has been given over the years or has had handed down from queens before her.

*

The amount of jewelry she has along with her at any one time might well be worth comfortably in excess of a million dollars. No wonder her staff were horror-struck when the whole lot unaccountably vanished during the lengthy world tour Elizabeth undertook following her coronation. She and Philip had been staying overnight at a small hotel in New Zealand. They were up early the following morning and off to Wellington, the New Zealand capital, leaving their servants behind to clear up and pack. As each case, bag, and box was packed, it was manhandled downstairs to be loaded onto the army trucks waiting outside. Except for the case containing Elizabeth's jewels. That would be taken to Wellington personally by one of her staff.

With the work of packing and loading almost done, the footman assigned to safeguard the jewel case went along to the royal bedroom to collect it. There was no sign of it. He looked under the bed, in the bathroom. Still no sign. Other royal servants joined in the hunt, looking in closets, along corridors, downstairs in the lobby. Had one of the army personnel sent along with the trucks perhaps taken it in error? There was a dash outside, but the trucks had gone.

The worried footman, along with Elizabeth's dresser and page, jumped into a car and set off after the trucks. They caught up with them at the local airport—just in time to see a plane take off with the royal luggage on board. They boarded another aircraft and flew in pursuit but touched down at Wellington only to find that the baggage plane had already been unloaded. They piled into another car and arrived at Government House just as the luggage was being unloaded from trucks and carried inside by army personnel. Springing from the car, the footman sprinted toward a stack of luggage still piled on the front steps. "I'll take that," he said to a soldier just about to pick up the large, inconspicuous case that held jewels worth a queen's ransom.

*

In New York on another occasion, it was Elizabeth's camera case that caused consternation. Her cameras travel with her in a zippered grip. The zipper had broken and, as a temporary measure, one of her staff had fastened the case with a piece of string. An eagle-eyed secret service man spotted the string as the camera case was being carried aboard Elizabeth's airplane for the flight back to Britain.

"Hey, you—what's that you've got there?" he demanded.

"It's the queen's cameras," said the footman carrying the grip.

"Tied with string?" the secret service man queried incredulously. "Bring it here. Put it down there. Carefully."

While one secret service man kept guard over the footman, another moved in, cautiously untied the string, and investigated the contents of the case.

"Well, it could have been a bomb," said one of them, as the royal cameras were returned to the footman and carried aboard the aircraft.

*

Despite the lengthy and meticulous planning that goes into every royal tour, things still go wrong on occasion. Elizabeth once found herself leaving Malta from a derelict wharf littered with rusty equipment and broken-down vehicles while the honor guard for her departure stood smartly to attention on another wharf that had been specially spruced up for the occasion. Similarly, she touched down at Dubrovnick in Yugoslavia to find that the national reception committee and the honor guard that should have greeted her were already on the way to Titograd, under the impression that her aircraft had been diverted there.

*

The legend of "Queen's weather"—that Elizabeth has sunshine wherever she goes—took a nasty knock in, of all places, California when she went there in 1983. Her visit to San Diego was marred by a downpour of rain. Her trip to President Reagan's ranch involved her in a twisting, seven-mile drive through swollen creeks cutting across a mountain road that had been partly washed away by freak storms. A planned horse ride with the president in the Santa Ynez mountains had to be abandoned, and instead of sailing from Santa Barbara to San Francisco in her splendid royal yacht, Elizabeth had to fly instead. "I knew we had exported many of our traditions to America," she joked, "but had not realized the weather was one of them."

*

Wherever the royals go, crowds turn out, bands play, flags are flown, and all sorts of diversions are staged to entertain them. Tribesmen in North Borneo decided to show Elizabeth and Philip how good they were with their blowpipes and poisoned darts. "Be careful, darling," Elizabeth cautioned her husband as he examined the weapons. "Remember that the arrows are tipped with poison." However, a subsequent demonstration of blowpipe efficiency fell rather flat. Despite a good deal of huffing and puffing on the part of a stalwart young warrior, no poisoned dart flew out of his blowpipe. "The thing is probably full of fluff," quipped Philip.

*

An entertainment staged for Elizabeth's benefit on Pentecost Island ended in tragedy. The young men of the island were displaying their skill and daring by skydiving from a seventy-foot tower with jungle vines tied to their ankles to pull them up just short of the ground. One vine broke under the strain, and the young skydiver hit the ground, killing himself, only feet from where Elizabeth stood watching.

In Japan it was thought that Elizabeth and Philip might like to see girl pearl divers at work. Japanese pearl gifts normally dive topless, but this, it was felt, might embarrass the queen. So a cover-up scheme was devised, with each girl being given a thin white cotton slip to wear while Elizabeth was around. But the normally efficient Japanese had overlooked one small fact: White cotton, when wet, is virtually transparent. In consequence, the scene when the girls came to the surface again after diving for pearls was like something out of a James Bond movie, their breasts clearly visible through the wet cotton. Elizabeth hurriedly averted her gaze, while Philip did a grinning double take.

*

Unable to afford the cost of new flags to fly on the occasion of a royal visit, the civic fathers of a small town in New Zealand decided to purchase a bundle of old naval signal flags. It was Philip, an ex-navy man himself, who first spotted the flags as he and Elizabeth drove into town. Chuckling, he translated for Elizabeth's benefit what the flags spelled out: "Danger—am loading high explosives."

*

In Britain especially, though occasionally elsewhere also, civic fathers often seem to suffer a rush of blood to the head at the news that the royals are coming their way. In one town, a row of derelict, deserted cottages had broken windows repaired and timberwork repainted because Elizabeth was no more than driving past them. The boarding used to patch up the broken windows was even painted with imitation blue curtains to give an impression of occupancy. At another place, where the royal train was due to make no more than a two-minute stop, twenty-two men were set to work to lay new paving stones, erect a new fence, and give the station buildings their first paint job in twenty years. And at a government research establishment

Elizabeth and Philip were to visit, four workmen spent two weeks installing new plumbing, new tiles, and repainting the lavatory.

Some of the things done when the royals are on the way are quaint in the extreme. The day Elizabeth visited the BBC headquarters in central London, nearby street signs pointing the way to the nearest public lavatories were dismantled and carted away. Up north, when Elizabeth went there on one occasion, a shopkeeper was told to switch off an illuminated sign in his window. It advertised contraceptives. Elsewhere, a street trader was told to cover up the sign displayed above his stall. It advertised "Juicy Hot Dogs." At a school being visited by Princess Margaret, five men were put to work felling saplings, carting them to the school, and then sticking them into the ground to conceal a collection of tumbledown huts. Elsewhere, a farmer was asked to move his cows to another field. The field they were in adjoined a rail siding in which Philip would be spending a night aboard the royal train.

*

Philip was full of admiration for the splendid new gymnastic equipment in use at one boys' club he visited. What he did not know was that, as soon as he had left, the equipment was loaded on a truck and returned to the school from which it had been borrowed in order to impress the royal visitor. Similarly, there was a splendid show of daffodils in the garden of an old people's center when Elizabeth's cousin, Princess Alexandra, went there. But like the gymnastic equipment at the boys' club, the daffodils were merely stage props to impress the royal visitor. They had been planted just before Alexandra arrived and were dug up again after she left to go back where they had come from.

An even more elaborate hoax was played on Elizabeth the day she opened a new business school in London. She was shown a lecture hall crammed with students and was suitably impressed. Then she was taken along to the library, filled with students poring over books. Finally, she was shown the bar, packed with students relaxing over their drinks. The school had quite a lot of students already, she must have thought. In fact, the school being new, the student body was actually small. To give the impression of a busy, well-attended institution, it had been arranged that what few students there were should dash quickly from lecture hall to library to bar while Elizabeth was being guided from one to the other by a more circuitous route.

*

Gimmicks designed to give Elizabeth a good impression of whatever place she is visiting are not confined to Britain. In Stuttgart, West Germany, when she went there, the local grass was given a brighter shade of green by spraying it with dye. And in Edmonton, Alberta, when Elizabeth and Philip went there for the Commonwealth Games, there was considerable perturbation when it was realized that the nearest lavatory was all of seventy paces from where the royals would be sitting. Adjoining seats were promptly removed, that part of the stadium underpinned with concrete to take the extra weight, and a special royal lavatory built—at a cost of $45,000.

*

Elizabeth should be aware that such things sometimes go on. She herself once saw the other side of the picture. It was during World War II when she was serving in the Auxiliary Territorial Service. One day the unit was inspected by its commandant, who also happened to be her aunt, the princess royal. "You've no idea what a business it's been,"

176

Elizabeth confided to Margaret afterward. "Spit and polish all day long."

*

While most of those who host Elizabeth go to considerable pains to ensure her comfort, there was one notable exception in recent years. Morocco's King Hassan was unable to overcome his traditional Islamic attitude toward women even when the woman concerned was Queen Elizabeth II. And his fear of assassination hardly improved things when Elizabeth visited his desert kingdom. Given her own indifference to danger, she was amazed at King Hassan's elaborate security precautions when she and Philip found themselves changing cars seven times during a desert motorcade. And she was not at all pleased when, at the end, Morocco's king retired to rest in an air-conditioned luxury trailer while she was left to sweat in a hot, dusty tent.

Money Matters

Taxwise, Elizabeth II is the most fortunate person in Britain. As queen, because taxes are levied in her name, she does not pay any. Even money accruing to her from her substantial private investments reaches her tax free. Nor is she required to pay road tax on her cars or to license her dogs, as her subjects must. And when she dies, her multimillion-dollar estate will pass to Charles without death duties being levied on it. As Elizabeth's son and heir, Charles does not have to pay income tax either. But because he would feel guilty at escaping scot-free while others have to stump up, he voluntarily surrenders part of his huge income to the treasury. In bachelor days he gave them half. But now that he is a married man and father he has cut back his voluntary donation to one quarter. Unlike his wife and eldest son, Philip does have to pay income tax. He is treated as self-employed, with expenses offset against income. He pays tax on the balance at the going rate.

*

As monarch, Elizabeth II receives an annual state allowance known as the Civil List. "Civil" is Parliament's way of underlining the fact that the monarch no longer has control over the army and navy. For 1985 the amount was $4,771,440 (calculated at an exchange rate of $1.20 to the pound). It all goes to paying her small army of retainers, feeding them, feeding the horses that draw the royal carriages, running her cars, holding garden parties, royal banquets, and the like. None of it goes into her own pocket.

*

As queen, Elizabeth also receives substantial perks. Her letters go through the mail unstamped. If her official residences, Buckingham Palace and Windsor Castle, require doing up, the state pays. She has the free use of the royal yacht *Britannia* and of a squadron of helicopters and aging aircraft known as the Queen's Flight. Total cost of it all in 1983 was $33 million. With the yacht requiring a $7.2 million refit, it will have been more in 1984. Others of the family also share in the perks. Margaret's ill-fated marriage to Tony Snowdon started with a honeymoon aboard the royal yacht. Anne and Mark and Charles and Diana similarly had the benefit of the yacht for honeymoon cruises. And when Charles and Diana flew to Liechtenstein for a skiing vacation early in 1984, they did so in one of Elizabeth's official aircraft. That ten-day holiday, including the hire of hotel rooms for the air crew and security men, is calculated to have cost Britain's taxpayers something in the region of $35,000.

*

Others of the family also receive generous annual allowances under the Civil List. Here are the 1985 figures (also calculated at an exchange rate of $1.20 to the pound):

Philip	$231,120
Anne	$144,000
Queen Mother	$414,360
Margaret	$140,160
Andrew	$ 24,000 (in addition to his naval pay)

*

Edward, the youngest of the family, should also have had $24,000 in 1985. But Elizabeth felt that he did not need that much while studying at university. So she arranged that he should have only $10,200, with the rest salted away to provide him with a small nest egg for the future.

*

Since 1969 these annual payments to the royals have been indexed to keep pace with inflation. Before that they had remained unchanged over the seventeen years since Elizabeth first became queen. In consequence, many of Elizabeth's staff were considerably underpaid, and it became almost impossible to balance the royal house-keeping accounts. "We are in the red," Philip proclaimed publicly when he appeared that year on American tele-vision. "I may even have to give up polo." The British embassy was promptly inundated with donations from generous Americans, London dockers organized a collection to subsidize Philip's polo playing, and a small boy pressed his 6 cents pocket money into Elizabeth's hand during the course of a royal walkabout. "It's to help your palace," he explained. Naturally, the embassy returned the American donations and the dockers were asked to give their collected money to a boys' club. But Elizabeth was so taken aback by the small boy's offering that she accepted it without quite realizing what was going on. It all served to shame Britain's government of the day into realizing that monarchy cannot be run on the cheap.

*

Two members of the family do not get official allowances. They are Prince Charles and the youngest of Elizabeth's Kent cousins, Prince Michael. Charles does not need an allowance. As heir to the throne, he is also the owner of the Duchy of Cornwall, an ancient royal estate that he inherited at the age of three. The first owner was the

Black Prince, back in the fourteenth century.

Despite its name, the estate is by no means confined to the county of Cornwall. It includes properties in six other English counties as well as parts of London and the Isles of Scilly (where Charles also has a hideaway holiday home). Its holdings are widespread and some of them curious—a tin mine and a granite quarry, oyster beds, a cricket ground, and a fast-food shop. If anyone dies in Cornwall without making a will, the money goes to Charles. So does the cargo of any ship wrecked on the Cornish coast and the carcasses of whales or porpoises washed up on Cornish beaches.

But income from such anachronistic sources is a mere fleabite compared to what the duchy makes from rents and property deals. Net profit in 1983–1984 was only a few dollars short of 1.5 million dollars (calculated at $1.20 to the pound). Of this, Charles drew a little over one million to pay his way as Prince of Wales and Heir Apparent. Though he is not legally required to pay income tax, he handed 25 percent voluntarily to the Treasury. The lowest rate for any other tax-paying Briton is 30 percent—and there is, of course, nothing "voluntary" about it.

As with his mother, there are substantial perks, too. Highgrove, the country mansion he bought when he married Diana, did not cost him a penny out of his own pocket. His Duchy of Cornwall bought it for him at a cost of around $1 million.

*

Having so much money sometimes "worries" him, he says. To quote him on the subject: "I could, I suppose—as it says in the Bible, as Christ stays—give it up.... 'Go and sell all you have and follow me.' But I am not sure how far that would get me in today's society. I think it would be a three-or-four-day wonder. A lot of people would think I was quite dotty, probably, and I am not sure how much I would achieve."

*

While Charles, with all the money he has coming in from the Duchy of Cornwall, hardly has need of a state handout, Elizabeth's cousin, Prince Michael of Kent, could do with one but doesn't get it. He might well have gotten one, as his brother and sister do, if he hadn't married a Catholic. Under British law, no Catholic can become queen. So Michael—a godson of President Roosevelt, incidentally— was obliged to renounce his right of succession to the throne. So there is no official allowance for him and his wife despite the number of public engagements they fulfill. "We'll go anywhere for a free meal," they joke. There were free meals aplenty and generous hospitality in other directions when they traveled to Rhode Island in 1983 for the America's Cup yachting races.

*

Michael and his wife live in the Royal Triangle, a small, pleasant rural area of England of which the other two corners are Highgrove, the country home of Charles and Diana, and Gatcombe Park, where Anne and Mark live. Their $360,000 home is reputed to be haunted by the ghost of a blacksmith who was hanged three centuries ago for sheep stealing, though the ghost has not been seen since Michael called in two local priests to bestow a "house blessing" on the property soon after he bought it in 1980.

*

While Michael does not get an official royal allowance, others among Elizabeth's cousins do, though in curious fashion. Michael's elder brother, Edward, Duke of Kent, along with their sister, Princess Alexandra, and another cousin, Richard, Duke of Gloucester, were down to receive a total of $410,000 among them in 1985. In fact, the money is given to them by Elizabeth herself, though indirectly so that they do not feel they are dependent on her charity.

183

Britain's government gives them the money, and Elizabeth gives it back to the government out of her private income.

*

For years the Kents were the church mice of the royal family, hard pressed for money after their father was killed in a wartime air crash. Edward, the eldest, was six at the time, Alexandra five, and Michael a baby of only seven weeks. Edward, though he immediately inherited his father's title of Duke of Kent, did not inherit his royal allowance. That had died with him, and the bulk of the family's small private fortune was locked up in a trust fund that no one could touch until Edward came of age. The children's mother could have had a meager air force pension of some $500 a year, but haughtily rejected it as "humiliating." Instead, she sold the family's elegant London home in fashionable Belgrave Square along with its antique furnishings and retired to live quietly and cheaply in the country. Her mother-in-law, Queen Mary, helped out financially. So did her brother-in-law, Elizabeth's father. He paid for the children's schooling. Even so, the widowed Princess Marina was obliged to lay off most of her servants, and her country home, with her little money to spend on it, gradually deteriorated around her. When the children were on holiday, she could no longer afford to take them to visit her sisters in Europe. Instead, they had to make do with the uncertain weather of the English seaside, booked in anonymously at small, cheap hotels as "Mrs. M. Kent and family." Unable to make ends meet, Marina was finally forced to sacrifice treasured family heirlooms—pictures, silver, antiques—which were disposed of through London auction rooms to raise money. Yet despite everything, she still managed to keep up appearances on royal occasions. She did so by obtaining dresses from leading fashion houses "on approval," wearing them for a royal ball or banquet, and returning them the next day. The fashion houses were happy to oblige. With her tall, slender figure, Marina was as much a royal fashion model in her day as Diana is now, and the fashion houses concerned were amply rewarded by the scores of other customers eager to buy copies of anything in which the Greek-born princess had been seen.

*

Except for Elizabeth's own children, there are no official allowances for the present generation of young royals. They have to work for their livelihoods. The Duke of Kent's delectable daughter, Lady Helen Windsor, is a trainee in the art department of a London auctioneering concern. Princess Margaret's son, David, Viscount Linley, is in the furniture business. Along with some former school friends, he has formed a cooperative that designs and makes desks, chairs, tables, cabinets. Charles and Diana bought one or two pieces for their new home from him, and Florida is proving a good export market. Between studying art and fashion design at a London college, Margaret's daughter, Sarah, works as a movie production assistant.

*

Others of the family make extra money as opportunity serves. Anne's husband, Mark, farms their country estate on a commercial basis. The couple also stage equestrian events, charging admission. Princess Margaret rents out her holiday home on Mustique. Pheasants shot by Philip at Sandringham are marketed at $5 a brace. Pigs are also reared there for bacon, milk sold to a nearby dairy, peas go for freezing and fruit for canning, all on a commercial basis. Elizabeth makes money breeding racehorses and polo ponies. She charges an admission fee to those wanting to see her country home at Sandringham and has a shop there selling tourist souvenirs. But she draws the line at renting out the royal yacht. A Canadian firm once offered $700,000

185

to charter it for a two-month cruise. "Certainly not," she said.

*

Among other things, Elizabeth has her own racetrack—at Ascot. It has been handed down to her from the days of stout Queen Anne. But this she operates on a strictly nonprofit basis.

*

When Anne and Mark married, Elizabeth's wedding gift to the couple—a country mansion and two farms—set her back around $1.25 million. The true extent of her wealth is a close-kept secret. Guesstimates have ranged from $3 million to $150 million. The difficulty in even estimating her fortune is in knowing what actually belongs to her as Elizabeth Windsor and what is hers only in trust as Queen Elizabeth II. Buckingham Palace and Windsor Castle, for instance, actually belong to the state. But Sandringham (20,000 acres) and Balmoral (80,000 acres) are her personal property. They were left to her by her father, who bought them from his eldest brother when he abdicated the throne to become Duke of Windsor. So are her racing thorough-breds, her stud stallions, and brood mares. So is the huge hoard of jewelry she has been given over the years, though not the Crown Jewels. The Crown Jewels, along with the royal store of gold plate (over five tons of it), a library of a hundred thousand rare books, antique furnishings that it requires seventy-five volumes to catalog—these things are hers only during her lifetime, held in trust for Charles, William, and all the kings and queens who will come after them. The same applies to the royal picture collection, with its hundreds of drawings by Leonardo da Vinci, over fifty Canalettos, at least twenty-six Van Dycks, to say nothing of paintings by Michelangelo, Raphael, Rembrandt, Rubens, Vermeer, and dozens more of the great masters.

The Crown Jewels, because they belong to the Crown in abstract rather than to Elizabeth herself, are not kept at Buckingham Palace but in a strong room at the Tower of London, where tourists, on payment of an admission charge, are permitted to view them. As well as crowns, scepters, and swords, the collection includes rings, bracelets, spurs, spoons, and salt cellars. Historically they are priceless, and even intrinsically they are worth a queen's ransom. One diamond alone of the 2,783 that glitter in the Imperial State Cown is a magnificent gem of 309 carats. Even bigger, at 516½ carats, is the diamond known as the Great Star of Africa which gleams in one of the royal scepters. Both stones were cut from the famous Cullinan diamond, a giant of 3,025 carats in its rough state. The Dutch diamond cutter charged with the task of cleaving it was so overawed by the prospect that he fainted. Revived and seated again at his bench, he succeeded in dividing the original stone into nine major gems, 96 smaller ones, and a number of so-called chips.

Also in the Crown Jewels collection is the crown made for Elizabeth's mother when she was crowned queen consort in 1937 following the abdication of her brother-in-law, the Duke of Windsor. Among the jewels adorning it is the legendary Koh-i-Noor diamond, said to bring good fortune to any woman who owns it but disaster to any man. It came into the possession of the royal family when the East India Company gave it to Queen Victoria. She nearly didn't get it. Given temporary charge of it, a certain Sir John Lawrence popped it into his waistcoat pocket and forgot all about it. When the time came to present it to Queen Victoria, he couldn't find it. It was later found tucked away in a box filled with buttons and beads. A servant had found it in the pocket of the waistcoat and had tossed it casually into the box, thinking it no more than an old piece of colored glass.

If the Crown Jewels are not actually Elizabeth's personal property, she still has a fabulous jewel collection of her own, partly inherited from queens who have gone before, partly items she has been given over the years, an Aladdin's cave of diamonds, rubies, emeralds, and pearls in the form of tiaras, necklaces, bracelets, brooches, rings, pendants, and earrings. Among her favorites are a triple string of pearls given to her by her grandfather, King George V; a sapphire-and-diamond brooch her father gave her on her eighteenth birthday; a necklace and bracelet made from diamonds given to her in South Africa on her twenty-first birthday; a diamond bracelet Philip gave her on their wedding day; and a brooch made from a huge rose-pink diamond, the size of a half-dollar, that the Canadian John T. Williamson dug up from his mine in Tanganyika and sent her as a gift. It took her another five years to find matching diamonds with which to surround the big one in the center, but since then she was worn the brooch frequently.

Her grandmother, Queen Mary, when she died left brooches, and earrings as well as an unusual set of pear-shaped diamonds her own mother had won years before in a German state lottery. Elizabeth also inherited from her grandmother what she calls "Granny's chips." Some chips! The leftovers from cleaving the massive Cullinan diamond, they range from a mere four carats to ninety-two carats and have been fashioned into a series of necklaces, rings, and brooches.

Gifts of jewelry at the time of her coronation and over the years since—pearls from Bahrain, rubies from Burma, emeralds from British Columbia, diamonds from Australia and Brazil—have swelled the collection to a size and value unequaled in the Western world. Elizabeth even has a pinafore fashioned from gold chain mail studded with sapphires and amethysts that was given to her during her 1979 tour of the Arabian Gulf.

*

Despite her great wealth, Elizabeth has a strong economic streak. When an evening gown wears out, she has the sequins and beads adorning it carefully removed so that they can be used again. She hates throwing anything away. When little Prince William first went to stay with his royal grandmother, she took him for airings in an old-fashioned, high-bodied baby carriage. She had first bought it when William's father, Prince Charles, was born, over thirty years before. And when Charles lost a dog leash while out at Sandringham on one occasion, she sent him out again to look for it. "They cost money," she admonished him.

Her economic streak stems from her childhood. As a small girl she had a weekly spending allowance of 1 shilling (equivalent to about 6 cents today). Later, when her father became king, this was increased to 5 shillings (30 cents). Small as her allowance was, there was little she could spend it on—she hardly ever went to the shops—and by the time she was thirteen she had £30 ($36) saved in her piggy bank.

She has raised her children in the same thrifty pattern. When Charles first went to boarding school she allowed him only a half crown a week spending money (about 15 cents). Anne had the same. Money went further in those pre-inflationary days, of course, and a shade further still in the days of her own childhood.

*

In consequence of their upbringing, Elizabeth's economic streak has rubbed off on her children. Andrew, in school-days, was once in the school pottery shop when another boy wiped his clay-smeared hands on the princely coverall. "Cut that out," Andrew said sharply. "It costs money to launder these things."

Anne, when she took part in the 1976 Olympics, flew economy class from London to Montreal just like an ordinary British athlete. Charles, when he was a student at Cambridge, once went out in search of a new necktie. Recognizing him, the shopkeeper produced a selection of pure silk ties for his consideration. "Too expensive," said Charles. In another shop, where he bought an umbrella, he was careful to check his change. "Excuse me," he said to the assistant, "but I think you've given me a pound short." With his careful, economic streak, it is no wonder that Diana's dress bills horrified him in their first year of marriage.

*

Financially, Prince Philip is a man who likes to stand on his own two feet. He always did. When he married Elizabeth he was a humble lieutenant whose annual naval pay ran to a modest thousand dollars or so. To help him live as befitted a member of the royal family, Parliament voted him another $12,000 a year. But Elizabeth, because she was Britain's future queen, got four times as much. He was not going to live on his wife's money, Philip insisted. But living on his money meant making do with so few servants that their butler, the first time they gave a house-warming party, complained that there was no one to do the washing up. Philip cheerfully detailed Elizabeth's detective body-guard to get busy at the sink. This was not at all the sort of thing Elizabeth was used to, and she pressed Philip into engaging two more footmen for the future. He could not afford them, so she paid.

*

Other males marrying into the royal family since have had the same sort of financial problems. At the time they were married, Anne's royal allowance was more than twelve times that of Mark's army pay. In consequence, he resigned from the army shortly after the wedding to run the two farms his royal mother-in-law had bought the couple as a wedding gift.

Not long before he married Princess Margaret, Tony Armstrong-Jones (as Lord Snowdon then was), an unknown and struggling photographer, went to a second-hand shop in search of a pair of riding boots. The cheapest he could find didn't match. "I'll take them anyway," he said. "No one sees both legs at the same time when you're on horseback." And even the small income he received as a photographer ceased abruptly for a time when he first married Margaret while his new royal in-laws debated whether it was dignified for him to continue working as a photographer. Eventually they decided that it didn't matter. Meantime, to tide him over, Margaret transferred part of her royal allowance to his bank account each quarter.

Out of his annual royal allowance, Philip pays the salaries of his aides and valets. He is a generous employer. Because he requires his aides to be available at all hours and sometimes at short notice, he thinks it is fair also to pay the rent of their London flats and their telephone bills.

The extent of Philip's generosity was clearly seen at the time of Elizabeth's coronation. Philip had commissioned the artist Felix Topolski to record the occasion in a set of murals. The work done, Topolski did not like to put a price on them, and Philip did not know what to offer. The Arts Council was asked to suggest a fee. They did so by measuring the size of the murals—382 square feet—and multiplying by four. The result, £1,582 (approximately $2,000), was to be Topolski's fee. Philip, when he heard how the figure had been worked out, didn't like it at all. "You can't pay an artist like Topolski as though he's a workman laying floor tiles," he remonstrated, and rounded the figure up to £2,000 ($2,400).

Out of his allowance, because he is still a man who likes to stand on his own feet financially, Philip also pays for the maintenance of the two royal cars he uses for public engagements and the wages of their chauffeurs. While his food and accommodation at the palace come free, he buys his own clothes, pays for his own laundry, and even buys the many thank-you gifts—cuff links, billfolds, and such—that he likes to distribute in the course of his worldwide travels. Much, if not all, of this expenditure ranks as business expenses, of course, and can be set off legitimately against his income tax.

*

When it comes to fund raising for charity, there are few better than Philip. Visiting Miami Beach on one occasion, he was offered $100,000 for his favorite charity if he would strip down and swim in someone's pool. He took the bet—and the charity got the benefit.

*

Compared with Elizabeth, Philip's childhood was an impecunious one. Hounded out of Greece, his parents were often forced to rely on the charity of relatives during their years of exile. When they wanted to sent Philip to an English-speaking school in Paris, they could not afford the fees. However, Douglas MacJannet, the school's American principal, took pity on them and waived any payment. Young though he was at the time, Philip never forgot his debt to MacJannet, and years later when he had married Elizabeth and she had become queen, he expressed his thanks by inviting his old master to a Buckingham Palace garden party.

Philip, in those days of the 1920s, went to school in clothes that were sometimes patched, sometimes darned. And there was one day of pouring rain when he was forced to remain after school hours until the rain let up. He had no raincoat. He was hoping relatives would give him enough money for Christmas to be able to buy one, he said.

Later school fees, when he went to boarding schools in England and Scotland were paid by his mother's Mountbatten relatives, and his naval pay at the time he and Elizabeth were betrothed was a modest $11 a week. His inheritance, when his father died in Monte Carlo, consisted of a signet ring, a shaving brush, and a few suits of clothes. He had the suits altered to fit him and the shaving brush given fresh bristles so that he could continue to use it.

*

In the aftermath of World War II, Philip's three surviving sisters and their German husbands were often hard pressed for money. His eldest sister, Princess Margarita, and her husband, Prince Gottfried, found it necessary to augment their income at one time by having paying guests to stay at their castle home and serving strawberry teas in the garden. When Elizabeth and Philip invited Margarita to be Anne's godmother, she replied that she could not afford the airfare to London. Philip sent her the money. Later, on flying visits to Germany, he would often take along bundles of discarded royal clothing for his sisters and their children.

*

Elizabeth, unlike Philip and their children, has hardly ever handled money. Her only real experience of paying on the spot for what she bought was in childhood when her nanny would take her out once a year to buy Christmas gifts for royal relatives. As a result, helping out at a charity bazaar shortly after she had become queen, she did not know what change to give people when they bought things from her stall, and her lady-in-waiting had to count it out for her.

Except for what she puts in the collection when she goes

to church on Sundays, Elizabeth never carries money. Charles, too, seems to have gotten out of the habit since quitting the navy. When he and Diana were asked to buy some raffle tickets at a school gala they attended, they had to borrow 75 pence (approximately 90 cents) from their detective bodyguard. Charles didn't win anything in the raffle, but Diana went home with a set of plastic knives and forks.

*

Diana has money of her own inherited from a trust fund established by her American great-grandmother, Frances Work. She came into her inheritance at the age of eighteen and spent $60,000 buying herself a flat in London. It proved to be a good investment. Two years later, when she married Charles, she sold it for double what she had paid for it.

Princess of Wales though she now is, Diana still likes to do her own shopping as in bachelor-girl days and will sometimes pop out of her country home to buy candy, magazines, or such small feminine items as a nail file. She has a sharp eye for a bargain, and on holiday at Balmoral Castle, spotting a sale sign as she drove through a nearby town, she stopped the car and slipped into the shop to buy a cut-price sweater.

But shopping as Princess of Wales is by no means as free and easy as it was in bachelor-girl days. There must always be an armed bodyguard along. And for Elizabeth the days are gone when she could slip out to a do-it-yourself shop and buy new wallpaper for a room she was having redecorated at Windsor Castle. Such excursions are now deemed too risky. Instead, she must send one of the servants to shop for her or, when it comes to buying gifts for relatives, have a selection of items sent to the palace from which to make a choice.

*

Shopkeepers and firms who supply Elizabeth II on a regular basis are granted what is known as "a royal warrant," a time-honored custom dating back to the days of Elizabeth I. Along with the warrant goes the right to display the royal coat of arms over the shop front, on delivery vehicles, products, notepaper, and—very discreetly—in advertisements. *Discretion* is the watchword. Any blatant publicity is firmly discouraged, and any firm so foolish as to boast of Elizabeth's patronage in a television commercial would quickly find themselves struck from her shopping list. Despite such stringent limitations, to gain a royal warrant is said to be "the finest advertisement money can't buy."

With a few more traders and shopkeepers winning their spurs each year, the list of royal-warrant holders now runs to several hundred names. They are particularly thick in London's West End—jewelers, hatters, shoemakers, fashion designers, along with shops selling Elizabeth's favorite brands of mint chocolates and toilet soap. There are others further afield, among them sword cutlers and the makers of footmen's livery, suppliers of nosegays and gold leaf, a Scottish maker of bagpipes, and even the firm that produces a brand of dog food favored by the royal corgis. Philip, Charles, and Elizabeth's mother also hand out their own warrants to their favorite firms and stores, as Diana will do also in due course.

Fashion Notes

Fashionwise, Diana found herself with a lot of catching up to do when she married Charles. Her wardrobe to that point had been the relatively modest one of the average bachelor girl who works for her living. Not that she could not have afforded more clothes had she wanted. Her father is well-to-do. In addition, at eighteen she had her own small fortune from a trust fund established by her American great-grandmother. Part of this went toward buying a flat in one of the best residential areas of London, which she shared with three other girls who paid her rent. Her comparatively modest wardrobe at the time, say her friends, was more because she had no special interest in fashion. As Princess of Wales, she was suddenly very interested indeed, and the first year of marriage saw her seeking expert advice from friends working on *Vogue* magazine, dashing around fashion salons, trying on clothes, tearing them off again, commissioning designs, and occasionally tossing in her own design ideas. It all cost a lot of money. Fashion designers, well aware of the prestige that would come their way once it was known that they were designing for the Princess of Wales, were—and are—more than willing to supply her at wholesale prices. Even so, a single exclusive ball gown— and she has dozens by now—could mean a bill for $1,200 or more. No wonder that Charles, wealthy though he is, looked askance as the bills mounted and her clothes buying over an initial twelve-month period set him back something like a cool $100,000.

*

Diana has her own favorite shops and fashion designers. Here are some of them:

- Dresses, suits, coats for public engagements—Bruce Oldfield, Jasper Conran, Jan Vanvelden, Victor Edelstein, Catherine Walker (of the Chelsea Design Company), Jacques Azagury, Belville Sassoon, Caroline Charles, David Neil and Julia Fortescue, Jean Muir
- Country clothes—Bill Pashley, who runs a one-man operation, designing, cutting, and stitching everything himself, in Battersea
- Maternity clothes—Joseph Conran and Global Expectations in the Fulham Road
- Off-the-peg dresses—Donald Campbell in Knightsbridge
- Blouses—Brother Sun boutiques
- Lambswool sweaters—Benetton stores
- Shirts (which she wears with jeans)—Charles' shirtmakers, Turnbull and Asher in Jermyn Street
- Hats—John Boyd, Viv Knowland, Graham Smith (for Kangol)
- Shoes—Edward Rayne in Bond Street
- Thermal underwear (for winter)—mail order from Damart
- Baby clothes—Please Mum in Bond Street
- Hair Styling—Head Lines in South Kensington.

*

"I'm a walking advertisement for Damart," Diana revealed once in one of her more gushing moments.

Certainly the feather-light thermolactyl underwear the firm produces enables her to make public appearances during the cold weather in outfits seemingly more suited to spring or summer. In America the firm operates from Portsmouth, NH, from where it sends out the masculine equivalent of Diana's warm, feathery underpinnings to football squads like the New York Jets, the Pittsburgh Steelers, the Philadelphia Eagles, and the Buffalo Bills.

*

Damart is not the only outfit for which Diana has become a walking advertisement since she burst upon the public scene as Princess of Wales. Even as she mounted the steps of St. Paul's Cathedral for her wedding to Charles, copycat designers, crouched in front of television sets, were busy sketching cut-price copies of her fantasy wedding dress. The British can work fast when they want to, and even as Diana and Charles were sitting down to their wedding breakfast in Buckingham Palace, the first rush-produced copies of the dress were already on display in store windows in London's Oxford Street.

In the first six months after the wedding, one firm alone sold over two hundred copies of the dress. Oddly, Arab brides in the Middle East were among the most enthusiastic buyers. In Britain, knickers, culottes, capes, and frilly blouses equally became feminine status symbols as young women rushed to the shops to model themselves on Diana. Hats, too, especially dainty hats with romantically misty veils, became all the vogue because of Diana's enthusiasm for them. Girls who had long gone bareheaded—as Diana herself did in her bachelor-girl days—suddenly surrounded themselves with a selection of boaters and platters, pillboxes and tricornes. It all gave Britain's hat trade a welcome 20 percent boost, with one firm stepping up production a staggering 50 percent until it was turning out 5,000 new hats a week.

*

In a country where so many people ape the royal family, baby William, too, has quickly become a fashion trendsetter. Photographs of him dressed in a navy-blue snowsuit with an embroidered *ABC* motif triggered off a frantic rush on the part of mothers eager to outfit their offspring similarly. Initially, most were disappointed. The store from which Diana bought the snowsuit had imported only a few dozen—they were made in France—and these were soon gone. However, astute copycat manufacturers were quick to jump on this new juvenile bandwagon. For some, it was simply a matter of hurriedly stitching almost identical *ABC* motifs on their own existing line of children's snowsuits.

*

Diana's elaborate wedding dress was made from forty yards of pure silk puffed out with one hundred yards of netting. To avoid the chance of anyone else turning out copies ahead of the actual wedding day, it was also made under conditions of cloak-and-dagger secrecy that would have done credit to James Bond. The actual design was kept locked in a safe with security guards keeping vigil at night. Even in daytime the window blinds were drawn before the design was brought out of the safe, with the work of cutting and stitching the dress done by artificial light.

To avoid upsetting either of her divorced parents, Diana, on her wedding day, wore the family tiara of the Spencers (her father's family) and a pair of diamond earrings that belonged to her mother. The fact that both items were borrowed also enabled her to conform to the wedding-day superstition that a bride should wear "something old, something new, something borrowed, something blue." The "something old" was a small piece of antique lace that had once belonged to Charles' great-grandmother, Queen Mary, while the "something blue" was a small blue bow stitched into the waistband of the wedding dress. The dress itself was the "something new," of course.

*

David and Elizabeth Emmanuel, who designed Diana's wedding dress, also designed the daringly low-cut and strapless dress in which she provoked oohs and ahs on her first-ever public engagement, accompanying Charles to the Royal Opera House in London in their courtship days. Charles himself loved the dress, but his grandmother, the queen mother, was heard to murmur that it was perhaps a trifle too revealing for a future Princess of Wales.

*

While her wardrobe has grown apace since she became Princess of Wales, it will be a long time before Diana can rival her royal mother-in-law's fabulous collection of jewelry. Still, she is off to a good start. Elizabeth herself has given her one of the royal family tiaras. Charles, at varying times, has given her a gold wristwatch, a gold bracelet, and a pearl choker. Among her wedding gifts was a set of diamond-and-sapphire jewelry cradled in a gem-encrusted gold box, a gift that set the oil-rich Crown Prince of Saudi Arabia back by some $300,000. Not to be outdone, the Emir of Qatar gave her another set of jewelry in gold, diamonds, onyx, and coral, while the Crown Prince of Jordan weighed in with a gold choker studded with precious stones.

*

If Diana is now the queen of British fashion, her husband is no slouch in matters of sartorial elegance. He has a wardrobe of nearly a hundred army, navy, and air force uniforms. He wears them, as appropriate, for functions involving any of the ten regiments in Britain of which he is either colonel or colonel in chief. As well as being a British colonel ten times over, he is also a commander in the navy, a wing commander in the air force, and colonel of some Canadian and Australian regiments, and he holds the rank of Air Commodore in Chief of the New Zealand Air Force.

Charles bought his first uniform at the age of nineteen when he was appointed Colonel in Chief of the Royal Regiment of Wales while still a university student. The appointment was made so that he could wear his new uniform for the minicoronation that saw him invested as Prince of Wales at Caernarvon Castle. He did not want any repeat of the embarrassment suffered by his great uncle, later Duke of Windsor, when he went through the same ceremony a generation before. Lacking a uniform, Windsor was obliged to wear white satin knee breeches and a purple surcoat trimmed with ermine. He thought it "a preposterous rig" and was worried that his young friends would laugh at him. "Your friends should understand that as a prince you are obliged to do certain things which may seem silly," his mother, Queen Mary, told him sternly.

*

Since Diana became her daughter-in-law, Elizabeth has sometimes copied her in matters of fashion. But what suits Diana is not always right for her mother-in-law. Diana has the advantage of height. She is a full six inches taller than Elizabeth and, in bare feet, only an inch shorter than Charles. So while Elizabeth always wears three- or four-inch heels to give the illusion of greater height on public occasions, Diana often restricts herself to the lowest of heels in order not to appear taller than her husband. For the joint photograph that appeared on one of the stamps specially issued by the post office to commemorate the couple's wedding, Charles stood on a box behind Diana.

*

Heights of the Royal Family:

Elizabeth	64 inches
Philip	71½ inches
Charles	71 inches
Diana	70 inches
Andrew	72 inches
Edward	72 inches
Anne	66½ inches
Queen Mother	62 inches
Margaret	62 inches

*

Elizabeth has never really cared for what she refers to as "dressing up and queening it." She is happiest when away from the public gaze and thus free to relax in well-worn tweeds and a pair of stout walking shoes. She has even been known to avoid wearing one of her several fur coats with the comment, "I don't want to look like a movie star." And the first time she saw her regal tiara and jewels laid out for her to wear in public as Britain's new queen, she was almost horrified. "I can't possibly wear all that," she protested.

"But you must, Lilibet," her loyal Scots dresser, Bobo MacDonald, insisted. "People expect it of you."

*

It is Bobo MacDonald's task, as Elizabeth's dresser, to look after her clothes and to ensure that the right outfit with its correct accessories is immediately at hand on all occasions. To assist her in this task she has the services of two assistants, and she needs them. Over her years of monarchy Elizabeth's wardrobe has mushroomed to such proportions that it now takes up three large rooms on the third floor of Buckingham Palace. In the corner of one room stands a mannequin made to Elizabeth's measurements on which a particular dress or robe can be draped for the

203

benefit of any artist commissioned to paint a new royal portrait.

Also in a place of honor in one of these wardrobe rooms is the most elaborate gown Elizabeth has ever worn—the one in which she was crowned queen. Not only is it the most elaborate of her many gowns but also the heaviest. Due to the crystal-and-pearl embroidery with which it is lavishly encrusted, it weighs an almost unbelievalbe thirty-five pounds.

*

Because Elizabeth has so little liking for "dressing up and queening it," there have been numerous arguments over the years as the loyal Bobo MacDonald has tried to persuade her to wear more striking clothes and Elizabeth has sought to cling to such tried-and-tested royal dresses as the traditional crinoline. It was only Bobo's insistence that finally persuaded Elizabeth to wear the clinging silvery evening dress that made her the rage of Paris on her first-ever state visit to France. Though she had had the dress made specially for the trip, at the last moment Elizabeth felt nervous about wearing it for a gala trip along the River Seine. She would wear a crinoline instead, she announced. Bobo argued in favor of the new dress, but it was no good. Elizabeth's mind was made up.

"Very well," Bobo said in the end. "Wear what you like, but don't blame me if you can't get up the gangplank of the river boat in a crinoline."

It was a telling point. With visions of perhaps having to be pushed and tugged up the gangplank in the voluminous crinoline, Elizabeth, however reluctantly, changed her mind yet again and decided to wear the new dress after all. Her appearance in it that night made her the toast of Paris.

*

For public appearances Elizabeth usually prefers to wear bright, clear-cut colors so that she can be easily seen at a distance and small hats that do not throw shadows across her face. Light summer dresses are sometimes weighted around the hem with small pellets so that high winds do not expose royal legs. She likes coats that button and a handbag that hangs from her wrist so that her hands are always free and available for hand shaking.

*

Tucked away in her handbag are her spectacles (she is farsighted), a handkerchief, her powder compact, and lipstick. No money. She never carries any. But she does carry with her a small, specially designed hook that she uses to hang the handbag just out of sight under the tabletop when eating.

*

In addition to her handbag, a zippered grip, carried around for her by her lady-in-waiting, travels with her wherever she goes. It contains the royal spares—spare pantyhose, a spare pair of shoes (in case she has the misfortune to break a heel), and several spare pairs of white gloves so that she can pop on a clean pair as soon as those she is wearing become soiled from hand shaking.

*

Elizabeth also takes a black mourning outfit with her wherever she goes, as indeed do all members of the royal family. The one time she did not have any mourning clothes with her—they had been sent on ahead to her next stopping place—was when her father died. She was in Kenya at the time and was forced to board her aircraft for the unexpected flight back to London wearing a light, bright summer dress. Yet when the aircraft touched down in London and she emerged into public gaze, she was dressed from head to toe in black as custom required.

In the meantime, when her aircraft had landed at a desert airfield in North Africa to refuel, Elizabeth had sent a radio message so that a second set of mourning clothes had been dispatched to the London airport to await her arrival. Her aircraft touched down initially at a distant part of the airport, and the new mourning outfit was sneaked aboard. Then, as the aircraft taxied slowly around to where Winston Churchill and the other top brass were waiting to greet the new queen, Elizabeth did a quick-change act into black.

But the mourning outfit she wore did not altogether meet with the approval of her grandmother, Queen Mary. "Much too short for mourning," she commented as she spied the length of her granddaughter's skirt.

*

The dresses Elizabeth wears for public functions start life as miniature watercolor sketches. Together with a sample of the material from which the dress or coat will be made, they enable her to judge how she will look in it. Once approved, her clothes are made under conditions of strict secrecy. Elizabeth is feminine enough—and queen enough—not to want to be confronted by dozens of mass-produced look-alikes when she appears on the public scene. Each new outfit requires several fittings, and the designer concerned goes along with his or her assistants to wherever Elizabeth happens to be—Buckingham Palace, Windsor Castle, Sandringham—at the time.

The state gowns Elizabeth has made for royal banquets overseas are elaborate in the extreme. Making and embroidering them is a long, time-consuming task. Each gown is designed and embroidered specially to honor the particular country she is visiting. Thus there was a design of maple leaves on the gown she had made to wear for a banquet in Ottawa, cornflowers and poppies on one she wore in Paris, cherry blossom in Tokyo, and mimosa in Australia.

Indoors, away from the public gaze, Elizabeth, to ease her feet, has a habit of walking around without shoes. Her fashion designers know that. So after each fitting an assistant always goes carefully over the carpet with a magnet to retrieve any stray pins.

*

The day dresses and coats Elizabeth has made for her overseas tours can be, and are, worn again for less important public functions back home in Britain. Her specially embroidered state gowns, each with its individual design, can never be worn again, of course. But Elizabeth insists that the embroidery be picked off and the pearls and crystal kept to be used again on a new dress. Despite her immense wealth, she is thrifty in the matter of clothes, as in most other things. A case in point was the yellow silk coat she had made for Charles' minicoronation at Caernarvon Castle. There was a change of fashion not long after, with the longer look becoming all the rage. Elizabeth promptly had the coat lengthened with a strip of matching embroidery tacked onto the hem.

And despite the size of her wardrobe, she was quick to add to it with a few cut-price bargains on her way to Japan. A stopover in Hong Kong, that home of lightning dressmaking, enabled her to have yet another evening dress plus a day dress and a matching coat run up for her overnight.

*

Unlike Elizabeth, her mother enjoys nothing so much as dressing in all her regal finery. The more pearls she has on, the more sumptuous her furs, the bigger her hat, the more she revels in things. She has a large collection of hats, most

207

of them big and ornate, many dripping with feathers, from which to make a choice for each public appearance. But she also has a few hats the public never gets to see, favorite old felts dating as far back as the 1920s, when she was a young and newly married duchess. She still wears them from time to time in private—for gardening. Her servants refer to them as "the queen mum's pea-picking hats."

Now in her eighties, Elizabeth's mother still keeps busy with public engagements. Indeed, next to Diana, she is without doubt Britain's favorite royal. The public adores her. But though she keeps busy, she takes no chances with either her health or the weather. Into her car with her whenever she sets out from Clarence House, her London home, goes a small wardrobe of clothes—tweed coat and raincoat, plastic overshoes, fleece-lined boots and spare pairs of shoes, umbrella, and a collection of head-scarves. To keep her warm in the car she has a fur rug and a foot muff, and, in really cold weather, even a hot-water bottle.

*

Other than by raising or lowering her hemline an inch or so, Elizabeth makes few concessions to current fashion. She would rather be comfortable than fashionable. For deer stalking in Scotland, she wears knickerbockers. She got the idea from her father. In fact, the first she ever wore, when she was a girl of twenty, were a pair of his, altered to fit her. Margaret teased her about looking "unfeminine" in them, but Elizabeth finds them eminently practical, and Diana agrees.

For occasions other than stalking, Elizabeth usually wears a tartan skirt when on vacation in Scotland. So does Anne. Philip, Charles, Andrew, and Edward all wear kilts. For skirts and kilts alike, they have the choice of several tartans—Royal Stewart, Hunting Stewart, or the red-and-gray Balmoral tartan, which Elizabeth's great-great-grandfather, Queen Victoria's beloved Prince Albert, designed for himself. If he is so minded, Charles can also wear the tartan of the Gordon Highlanders. He is their colonel in chief.

Philip, when he first went to Scotland in the days when he was courting Elizabeth, did not own a kilt. Elizabeth's father obligingly lent him one. On Philip, because of their difference in height, the king's kilt looked rather like a miniskirt. The family roared with laughter when Philip first appeared in it, and he responded by bobbing a mock curtsy.

Charles had his first kilt when he was a small boy. The result was a considerable tussle with his nanny. She wanted him to wear underpants beneath his new kilt. He objected. "Why should I wear them?" he demanded. "Papa doesn't."

*

Today's young royals are as with-it as anyone else of their generation in the matter of clothes. Diana wears a bikini for sunbathing. The Duke of Kent's daughter, Lady Helen Windsor, goes further. She has been known to sunbathe topless. Andrew was once refused admission to a London nightspot because he was not wearing a necktie. Called to the scene, the club's manager unearthed a spare tie from somewhere and lent it to Andrew. Princess Anne, in her younger days, wore a miniskirt to greet Richard Nixon when the American president visited Buckingham Palace. The fact that Anne wore a miniskirt so often in those days created something of a problem when she was due to visit a young farmers' club. The visit involved climbing an open-tread staircase. To preserve Anne's modesty, the staircase was hurriedly boarded over beneath.

*

The idea of one of his descendants wearing a miniskirt while another sunbathes topless would have horrified Elizabeth's great-grandfather, King Edward VII. He was a

209

stickler for correct dress. An admiral's daughter once arrived for a royal dinner party wearing a dress that ended no more than an inch or so above her ankles. To her embarrassment, the king reprimanded her, "I think you have made a mistake. This is a dinner party, not a tennis party."

The tuxedo, incidentally, owes its existence to Edward VII's fussiness about clothes. He had wanted to pursue a military career, but his mother, the autocratic Queen Victoria, would not allow it. So Bertie turned his enthusiasm for military uniforms to designing one of his own, which men friends were expected to wear when they dined with him. It consisted of black trousers, a black bow tie, and a short dark-blue jacket—the first tuxedo.

Royal Memoirs

That Elizabeth would grow up to be a conscientious and dutiful queen and Margaret an unpredictable and head-strong princess who defied convention, was clearly fore-shadowed in childhood. As a child, Elizabeth was neat and tidy, serious and thoughtful, disciplined and obedient, while Margaret was a harum-scarum girl, always teasing and laughing, getting into scrapes. Given candy, Elizabeth would count hers out, sort it into piles, ration herself to make it last, while Margaret would cram hers into her mouth by the handful. A dolls' tea party would see Elizabeth carefully wash and dry the miniature tea things afterward. Asked to help—or ordered to by their nanny—Margaret would conveniently disappear. At bedtime, Elizabeth would tidy away her toys and fold her clothes neatly while Margaret would leave hers strewn around.

Yet, curiously, it was Elizabeth who staged the biggest rebellion in childhood. Fed up with reciting French verbs in their nursery schoolroom one day, she grabbed her ink pot, held it aloft, and poured the contents all over her blond curls.

It was Elizabeth, too, who emerged from the palace shrubberies on another occasion coated in slime and dripping with water. She had been trying to see if there were any eggs in a ducks' nest and had fallen into the lake. Years later, Charles, in boyhood, returned to Windsor Castle one day equally wet and smelling foul. He had been helping with the sheep and had fallen into the sheep dip.

*

Even as a small girl Elizabeth was mad on horses. She collected toy horses as eagerly as other girls collect dolls. Asked what she wanted for Christmas or a birthday, it was invariably "another horse, please." At its peak her collection of toy horses numbered more than thirty. She "stabled" them on the landing outside her bedroom and meticulously "groomed" them each night before going to bed. They were still there on the palace landing the day she married Philip; she was twenty-one at the time. Today she has a similar collection of glass and china horses, which she "stables" in a cabinet in the sitting room she also uses as a study.

*

So that Elizabeth, in childhood, should have the company of more girls of her own age, her parents arranged for her to join the Girl Guides, though not quite in the usual way. A special Girl Guide company was formed for the purpose, other girls to join it were selected with care, and it was arranged that the weekly meeting would be held at Buckingham Palace. Perhaps not unnaturally, the parents of the other girls drew a wrong conclusion from all this. When the first meeting was held, they brought their daughters along to the palace not in traditional Guide uniform, but in their best party dresses.

*

Elizabeth was thirteen and Margaret nine when their parents visited the United States in 1939. President Roosevelt very much wanted the royal parents to bring the girls, too. "I shall try to have one or two small Roosevelts of approximately the same age to play with them," he wrote to Elizabeth's father. But King George VI wrote back, "They are much too young for such a strenuous trip."

*

Philip was a bit of a young rip in boyhood. He knocked out one of his teeth jumping from a hay wagon and lost another when he crashed while roller-skating. On one occasion in boyhood he bicycled seventy miles to a scout camp. Not wanting to cycle all that way back again, he hitched a ride on a barge. The barge was loaded with grain, and he slept overnight on the grain sacks. Staying with his Mountbatten relatives in England during school holidays, he would sneak out of the house at night with his cousin David. The two of them would make their way to the Hotel de Paris, a fashionable nightspot overlooking the Thames, and climb up on the roof so that they could watch the floor show through a skylight. Another time the police caught him just as he was clambering onto the roof of Kensington Palace. He was simply visiting his grandmother (who lived there at the time), he explained.

Another school holiday was spent with a family of Greeks, exiled like his own parents from their native country, at their villa in France. While he was there he saw a Persian carpet seller going from door to door with his wares. It gave Philip an idea. With the help of his host's young son, Ianni Foufounis, he rolled up two of the carpets in the villa and set off to try and sell them. Fortunately, the loss was discovered and the carpets retrieved before a deal had been struck.

*

Ianni Foufounis and his sister Helene (later well known in Britain and France as the singer Helene Cordet) were close friends of Philip in childhood. The two of them were living in England with their mother when Helene was married. Because they knew so few other people, they asked Philip, a teenager at the time, to be best man at the wedding. It was only when the wedding day was almost upon them that they realized that they had made no arrangements for someone to give the bride in marriage. Philip promptly volunteered to do that, too, and even offered the use of his grandmother's car to get the bride to the church on time. Solemnly he escorted the bride from car to church. Suddenly, at the very entrance to the church, she came to an abrupt standstill.

She was merely suffering from an attack of wedding-day nerves, Philip decided, and, being Philip, was confident of his ability to handle the situation.

"Move," he orderd her.

"I can't," she said.

"Yes, you can," Philip insisted.

"Not until you get off my train," Helene informed him.

*

However much of a wit and joker he has become since, Charles, in childhood, was like his mother before him, a quiet, serious, even rather nervous youngster. Anne was like Margaret born again, always on the go, always laughing, singing, and teasing. "Much the more forceful child," their old nanny remembers. Even a tantrum child at times if she could not get her own way. There was one day when she went into a tantrum because her nanny wanted her to wear an extra woolly and she did not want to. Philip, hearing the fuss that was going on, intervened to pop her over his knee and spank her. Charles, too, was once spanked in childhood for making faces from a window at sightseers gathered outside.

Like most kids, Charles and Anne went through a cowboy-and-Indian phase, charging around with toy guns clutched in their hands, startling servants with yells of

"Stick 'em up." For a time, westerns were their favorite TV diet (Anne still enjoys them), and Charles was nicknamed "Hopalong Cassidy" by his sister when he injured a leg and was obliged to hobble around in a plaster cast.

Charles in those days was nervous of horses, and one of Anne's favorite tricks, when the two of them were riding together, was to lean over and give her brother's mount a slap on the rump. Off it would gallop, with Charles clinging on for dear life while Anne roared with laughter. Anne has always been completely at home in the saddle. On vacation at Balmoral Castle one year, a series of ear-splitting whoops and yells caused Elizabeth to dash to the nearest window. Anne, wearing an Indian headdress she had been sent from Canada, was galloping around and around the lawn—bareback. "It's the way Indians ride," she shouted at her mother by way of explanation. "Never mind how the Indians ride," her mother called back. "Take that pony back to the stables this instant and put a saddle on it."

*

Given a pet lovebird apiece by their grandmother around this time, Charles and Anne decided to name them Davy and Annie (after Davy Crockett and sharpshooting Annie Oakley). They named their corgi pups Whisky and Sherry. For a time Charles also had a pet rabbit named Harvey and a pet hamster, which, for some reason, his mother disliked. "That horrible rat," Elizabeth called it. Diana, as a child, also kept hamsters and guinea pigs as pets. Her favorite guinea pig, which she even took to boarding school with her, was called Peanuts. Thrilled beyond words the day Peanuts won a prize in a local pet show, she threw her arms around the judge's neck and kissed him.

At Buckingham Palace, royal parents and children alike were enthralled the year a stray pigeon built a nest on the window ledge of one of the state rooms and proceeded to lay a clutch of eggs. Elizabeth, indeed, was so concerned for the bird that she gave instructions for the curtains to be drawn across the window and the pigeon left undisturbed until the eggs had hatched.

*

Anne's birthday, being in August, invariably finds the family on vacation at Balmoral Castle, where birthday parties in childhood often took the form of an outdoor barbecue in the heather-clad hills. There was one birthday for which Anne was given a new bicycle. Eager to ride it, she was permitted to follow behind the others on her new bicycle when the family set off for the customary barbecue picnic. But the end of the day found her too tired to cycle back, and her father volunteered to ride the bicycle back to the castle for her. Anne and the rest climbed into the Land Rover and were soon out of sight. Philip mounted the bicycle and pedaled after them. Unfortunately, his man's weight proved too much for the small child's cycle. He had not gone far when it collapsed under him and he was forced to footslog the rest of the way back to the castle with the ruined bicycle slung across his shoulders.

*

Andrew was three when Elizabeth found herself pregnant with Edward. To prepare him for the new arrival, she told him that he would soon have a little brother or sister as a playmate. Childlike, Andrew muddled this small piece of information and charged back to the nursery to tell his nanny that he was soon going to have "a baby brother *and* a baby sister." It was around this time, too, that a visitor to the palace asked him how old he was. "Three and a big bit," Andrew replied proudly.

Like most boys, Andrew was constantly getting into scrapes in childhood. There was one occasion when

Elizabeth, just about to leave for a public function, put her hat down on a convenient chair. Called away for a few moments, she returned to find Andrew punting the hat around the room like a football. There was another occasion when he could not resist trying on the tall bearskin his father wore as a colonel of the Welsh Guards. It was much too big for him, of course, and he ended up with it pulled right down over his face—and then found he could not get it off again. His ears had jammed in the wire framework on which a bearskin is mounted, and it required a deal of painful tugging to free him.

*

By curious coincidence, both Diana and her predecessor as Princess of Wales, the princess who later became Queen Mary, were educated at the same boarding school, West Heath. Diana, when she left school, took a Cordon Bleu cookery course. That done, she put her name down with an agency that got her various short-term jobs as baby sitter, mother's helper, and cook and washer-up for other people's parties. At the time Charles courted her she had two jobs. One was at a London kindergarten where she taught dancing and painting; the other was looking after the small son of Patrick and Mary Robertson, a New York couple living in London.

*

Of all the royal family, Elizabeth's mother is far and away the most philosophical, as was clearly seen the year she entered her horse, Devon Loch, for the Grand National, Britian's toughest steeplechase. Devon Loch's jockey was Dick Francis, better known today as the best-selling author of racing thrillers. Riding with great skill, Francis nursed Devon Loch over the thirty stiff jumps that brought so many other riders and horses to grief, and with the winning post less than a hundred yards away, was a clear fifteen lengths in the lead. A great roar went up from the crowd at the prospect of such a popular royal victory. As it did so—perhaps *because* of the roar of the crowd—a strange thing happened. Devon Loch suddenly leapt into the air as though trying to clear a jump that wasn't there and came down spread-eagled with Francis still in the saddle. And there it stayed until it had been passed by every other horse still left in the race.

Disappointed though Elizabeth's mother was, she gave a philosophical shrug of her plump shoulders. "That's racing for you," she sighed and went off to commiserate with both horse and jockey. "You rode a beautiful race," she told Francis and gave Devon Loch a consoling pat. "You poor dear old thing," she said to him.

*

Elizabeth's mother was philosophical, too, the evening of a royal dinner party when a footman, bending over from behind her with a tureen of vegetables, clean forgot about the gravy boat he was holding in his other hand. As he bent forward, the gravy boat tilted and hot gravy cascaded down the back of the queen mother's neck. Calmly she carried on conversing with guests as though nothing had happened. At the end of the evening the embarrassed footman sought her out and aplogized profusely. "Don't worry about me," she reassured him. "But perhaps you should apologize to my dreser. She's going to be rather upset about my dress."

*

There was another royal dinner party at which almost everything went wrong. Elizabeth's father, turning to speak to the guest seated immediately beside him, cracked his head on a meat platter one of the servants was holding. Later, a footman dropped a serving spoon on the table with such a clatter that the king almost jumped out of his chair. The final straw came as the cheese board was being carried around. As it passed behind the king, the cheese knife slid off the board and stabbed the king in the back of the neck. "Now they're bloody well trying to kill me," he boomed at the top of his voice.

*

Perhaps the strangest thing of all was what happened the night before Elizabeth's father died. Elizabeth and Philip were away in Kenya, engaged on a royal tour her father was too ill to undertake. The king and queen, as Elizabeth's parents were then, were at Sandringham, their country home. With them were their small grandchildren, Charles, three at the time, and Anne, a toddler of barely eighteen months.

Because he was too ill and weak to climb stairs anymore, the king had had a bedroom made up for himself on the ground floor. So it came as a surprise to the children's nanny when, that evening of February 5, 1952, he appeared suddenly in the doorway of the nursery, higher up in the house.

The children were having supper at the time, and their grandfather joined them. Supper over, he helped to tuck them into bed and said prayers with them.

It was the first time he had climbed the stairs to the nursery in all the six weeks the children had been at Sandringham. It was almost, some of the family thought later, as though he had had a premonition that he would never see them again. A few hours later, in the middle of the night, he died in his sleep.

War Diary

Like every other family in Britain, the royals played their part in World War II, had their share of triumph and tragedy. In many ways, they were almost a typical wartime family. During the course of the war Elizabeth:

- lost an uncle who was killed when his aircraft crashed
- had another uncle wouned by a German dive-bomber
- had a cousin taken prisoner during the Allied offensive in Italy
- was delighted when her sweetheart (Philip) was decorated for bravery at sea
- was relieved that Philip's uncle was among those saved when his destroyer was sunk with the loss of 130 lives
- had her home (Buckingham Palace) bombed

*

The uncle killed was the Duke of Kent's father, George, a Royal Air Force group captain serving on the staff of the inspector general. The uncle wounded was the Duke of Gloucester's father, Harry, a professional soldier who went to France on the outbreak of war, with the British

221

Expeditionary Force. The cousin captured was another George, now Earl of Harewood, who was serving with the Grenadier Guards. His brother Gerald was also in the Grenadiers. Their mother, the Princess Royal, fulfilled a triple role as head of the Red Cross, the Royal Air Force Nursing Service, and the Auxiliary Territorial Service. Another aunt, Princess Marina, widow of the dead George, led a curious double life in wartime. As Princess Marina, she was head of the Women's Royal Naval Service; as "Nurse Kay," she worked anonymously in a London hospital. Philip was in the navy throughout the war, seeing service in the Mediterranean and the Far East. Two of his uncles and a cousin were also in the navy. One of the uncles was Earl Mountbatten, later Supreme Allied Commander in South East Asia. Elizabeth herself, toward the end of the war, served for a short time in the Auxiliary Territorial Service.

*

Earlier on, Elizabeth was far too young to play any real part in Britain's war effort. She was only thirteen when war broke out and, childlike, would hurl a cushion at the radio set whenever the voice of "Lord Haw-Haw," Germany's English-speaking propagandist, came on the air.

*

The outbreak of war found Philip in a curiously anomalous position—a Greek prince, and therefore supposedly neutral, serving as a midshipman in Britain's Royal Navy. To get him out of the way, navy authorities packed him off to the Far East, where there was as yet no war. Even there, ship's captains did not want the bother of having a neutral Greek prince on board, and he found himself being unceremoniously shuttled from ship to ship. But the Italian invasion of Greece meant that he was no longer a neutral. He immediately applied to be sent where the action was. As a result, he found himself aboard a battleship in the Mediterranean on the night Britain annihilated the Italian fleet. Four Italian cruisers and two destroyers were sunk, and a battleship and another cruiser severely damaged, all this without a single casualty on the British side. For his part in the action—he was in charge of the searchlights so essential to a night engagement—his native Greece decorated him with the War Cross.

*

In 1940, when Elizabeth was fourteen and Margaret ten, the Germans, having already overrun much of Europe, began planning Operation Sea Lion—the invasion of Britain. Because they never succeeded in achieving mastery of the air, Operation Sea Lion never got off the ground. But the possibility of invasion was very real at one time, and it was suggested that Elizabeth and Margaret should be sent to Canada for safety. Their mother turned the idea down flat.

*

At the height of the German air blitz on London, with much of the city knocked flat by bombs, Elizabeth and Margaret were sent to Windsor Castle so that its massive stone walls might afford them greater protection. When the siren sounded to warn of a German air raid, the girls were told, they must go immediately to the castle dungeons. The first time this happened was at night. To the dismay of those responsible for their safety, Elizabeth firmly refused to go to the dungeons in her nightwear. She must be "properly dressed," she insisted. To speed things up during later air raids, her parents had one-piece "siren suits" made for their daughters, which they could slip on quickly over their nightdresses.

*

Child though she was, Elizabeth did what she could toward Britain's war effort. She went out collecting scrap metal that could be melted down and turned into armaments. She wrote cheerful girlish letters to royal servants who were fighting in the armed forces. She knitted "comforts" to send to them and to various royal relatives. Unfortunately, she was never much good at knitting, and a pair of socks she sent Philip were so shapeless as to be almost unwearable.

*

One September afternoon in 1940, when the air war over Britain was at its height, Elizabeth witnessed a dogfight between German and British planes over Windsor. It ended when the German plane was shot down and crashed in the castle park. To this day, over forty years later, Elizabeth recalls the incident "vividly," she says.

*

Elizabeth's parents also retreated to Windsor Castle to sleep most nights. But daylight always found them back at Buckingham Palace, at that time in the front line of the air war between Britain and Germany. They were there the day the palace was hit by German bombs. Watching from a window, they actually saw the bombs leave the German aircraft. They ducked immediately under the nearest table, crouching there while a stick of six bombs straddled the palace from front to back. The royal chapel received a direct hit and was destroyed. "I am glad we have been bombed," Elizabeth's mother said afterward. "Now I shall feel that we can look the East End in the face." The East End was the part of London that suffered most from German bombing.

Despite their narrow escape, Elizabeth's parents continued to work at the palace each day, the royal standard flapping above it. The windows of the king's study, shattered when the palace was bombed, were boarded over with timber. Royal aides wanted him to go on using the same room, working by artificial light. Then there would be no danger of being wounded by flying glass in the event of another air attack on the palace, they pointed out. Elizabeth's mother thought it a terrible idea. "We must be able to see the sunlight," she said and insisted on moving to another part of the palace, into a room with undamaged windows.

*

Both parents worked tirelessly and ceaselessly for Britain's war effort. Both learned how to handle a handgun and a Sten gun in case the Germans invaded. Together they visited the bombed cities of Britain to comfort the injured and the bereaved. To boost national morale, they visited shipyards and munitions factories, army and air force bases, ships of the navy, and later, when America entered the war, U.S. air bases in Britain. In secret Elizabeth's father also flew overseas to visit troops on the battlefronts in France, North Africa, and Malta. In World War I it had been the custom that only commissioned officers received their medals from the king. Elizabeth's father insisted on presenting every medal personally, whomever it was awarded to. He even had a lathe installed at Windsor Castle so that, in what little free time they had, he and his aides could make spares for military vehicles. At both Windsor and Buckingham Palace he ordered a black line painted on all baths, six inches up from the bottom. To conserve fuel, hot water must not be used above that level, he said. But while he himself rigidly observed his own fuel-saving rule, not all the servants did the same.

*

Among his war souvenirs Philip has a certificate that proclaims him to be a "qualified coal trimmer." He was awarded it when a bunch of Chinese stokers deserted ship

225

in Puerto Rico. Philip was among those who volunteered to man the stokehole and fuel the ship's boilers in their place. A man who will try anything once, he filled in a spot of shore leave on another occasion by working as a jackaroo— an Australian cowboy—on a cattle station in Queensland.

Philip was back in the Far East, now first lieutenant aboard the destroyer *Whelp*, when Japan surrendered. September 2, 1945, found him aboard Admiral Halsey's flagship, the *USS Missouri*, when his Mountbatten uncle, as Supreme Allied Commander, insisted on the defeated Japanese generals handing over their swords in token of their surrender.

*

Of all the royal relatives, it was surely Philip's mother who had the biggest cross to bear during World War II. While her son and two of her brothers fought for Britain, her three surviving daughters were all married to Germans. Indeed, one of them, Philip's youngest sister, Sophie, was widowed when her first husband, Prince Christopher of Hesse, was killed while flying with the Luftwaffe in Italy.

When the Germans overran Greece, most of the Greek royals fled the country. But not Philip's mother. She saw it as her duty to stay and help Greece. She had already sold her jewelry to aid the Greek war effort. Now she did hospital work and set up a sanctuary for Greek war orphans.

There was one occasion when the German commander in Athens, aware of her royal connections, called upon her to ask if there was anything he could do to make life more comfortable for her. "Yes," said Philip's mother curtly. "You can withdraw."

*

At the age of sixteen, Elizabeth, like every other youngster in wartime Britain, was required to register for war work. However, she was not sent to work in a munitions factory or a shipyard. Her father considered it more important that she should be trained to take over from him if he were killed, as his brother George had been. As heir to the throne, Elizabeth found herself deputizing for her father while he was away visiting British troops overseas. She visited British army bases and American air bases in Britain, and she launched a new battleship. At one American air base she named a new Flying Fortress. She gave it the name *Rose of York* and was saddened when she heard later that it had been shot down during a raid on Berlin. She visited coal mines, factories, and dockyards and was taken secretly to watch one of the rehearsals for the D Day landings.

But she never felt that she was doing enough and constantly plagued her father to let her join the armed forces. Her mother supported her pleas, and finally her father gave way. So she donned uniform as a second subaltern in the Auxiliary Territorial Service. She trained near Windsor and returned to the castle each night to sleep. To this extent she was featherbedded. But there was no featherbedding where her army training was concerned. By the time the war ended she could drive a heavy truck, change a flat tire, adjust a carburetor, grind valves, and decarbonize a cylinder head.

*

So that she could deputize for her father more effectively where her duties as a princess (as distinct from an army subaltern) were concerned, she was given her own car and provided with the services of a lady-in-waiting who accompanied her on her official visits to bases, factories, dockyards. Her lady-in-waiting proved to be one of the new breed of wartime women who were happier in a head-scarf than a hat. Elizabeth's mother was horrified. "You must

227

speak to her," she told Elizabeth. "She must wear a hat."
But Elizabeth merely laughed. "Don't be so old-fashioned,
mummy," she said.

*

Like his daughter, Elizabeth's father never felt he was
doing enough for Britain's war effort, though he did much—
and the strain was to shorten his life. "He feels so much not
being in the firing line," Elizabeth's mother confided in her
mother-in-law, Queen Mary. So when Winston Churchill,
Britain's wartime prime minister, declared his intention to
sail with the Allied invasion fleet on D Day, Elizabeth's
father thought it a splendid idea and decided he would go,
too.

Churchill was thrilled. "It will be a fine thing for a king to
lead his troops into battle as in the old days," he told the
king.

But if Churchill was thrilled, the king's principal personal
adviser, Sir Alan Lascelles, was horrified. A chance
German bomb or shell could mean the deaths of both of
them, leaving Britain with an eighteen-year-old queen and
no prime minister.

Elizabeth's father, as Lascelles knew from long
experience, could be an obstinate man. Telling him that he
shouldn't go to France on D Day would simply make him
more determined to go than ever. Lascelles wracked his
brain for a solution and finally settled upon a cunning ploy.

He went to see the king. "Before you depart on this
expedition, Your Majesty," he said, "perhaps you would
inform me as to what advice you would like me to give the
new queen concerning her choice of a new prime minister in
the event that neither you nor Mr. Churchill returns safely."

Not a word there suggesting that the king should not go.
But Elizabeth's father took the point and immediately
drafted a message to be sent to Churchill: "You said

yesterday that it would be a fine thing for a king to lead his troops into battle as in the old days. But if a king cannot do this, it does not seem right to me that his prime minister should take his place."

The king's message reached Churchill just as he was about to leave for General Eisenhower's headquarters. Rumbling, he sat down again and drafted a reply to be sent to the king. He would, he wrote, "defer to Your Majesty's wishes and, indeed, commands."

So the D Day invasion fleet sailed without either of them.

*

A child of thirteen when war broke out, Elizabeth was a young woman of nineteen when it ended. On VE night she and Margaret slipped secretly out of the palace to mingle anonymously with the celebrating crowds in London's streets. One of their escorts on that once-in-a-lifetime excursion was Group Captain Peter Townsend, the Battle of Britain fighter ace with whom Margaret was later to fall in love. But Margaret that night, not yet fifteen and immature for her age, had no thoughts of love. But she did have "great fun knocking people's hats off," she told her parents when they got back to the palace.

Close Encounters of the Royal Kind

Cocooned as she is within the high walls and tall railings of Buckingham Palace, surrounded by a small regiment of royal aides and palace servants, cushioned in the luxury of her specially built $72,000 Rolls-Royce or her own train whenever she sets foot outside, paying no income tax, Elizabeth II has little, if any, conception of what ordinary life is really like. She may know a Rubens from a Rembrandt as she studies the royal art collection or be able to recite the pedigree of a royal racehorse back through six generations, but she would be stumped if asked the current price of a pint of milk or a loaf of bread.

She was thirty-two before she ever dialed a telephone. She did it then only because royal duties required her to inaugurate Britain's new long-distance dialing system. It is doubtful if she has ever repeated the experience. At the palace, someone always makes her calls for her. She comes on the line only when the person to whom she wishes to speak has actually been contacted.

Similarly, in the early days of her reign, she once acted as volunteer saleswoman at a charity function held on her Balmoral estate in Scotland. But she had no knowledge of money, and her lady-in-waiting had to count out any change for her.

But if she knew nothing of money on that occasion, she was alive to the value of a diamond love-knot brooch she was wearing at the time. The brooch was clipped to her coat, which she removed at one point while serving the crowd of buyers besieging her stall. Another seller, thinking the coat was among the sales goods, was in the process of disposing of it for a few dollars, when Elizabeth realized what was going on. "Hey, that's my brooch!" she exclaimed, grabbing the coat back.

*

That Elizabeth should know almost nothing of everyday life is understandable. All her life she has been shielded from contact with the real world. Her only experience of schooldays was a weekly chauffeur-driven journey to Eton College where she was the only child in a class of one for lessons in constitutional history. Her only experience of shopping was when she was taken out by her nanny to buy gifts for relatives at Christmas time. She has sampled ordinary travel only twice in her life, again in childhood. Her nanny once took her for a short trip on a London bus and, on another occasion, for a ride on an underground train.

The train journey was followed by tea in a YWCA canteen, where she and nanny stood in line to be served. The whole business thrilled Elizabeth so much that she began to march off with her tray before a teapot had been put on it. Not recognizing her, the canteen assistant called out, "If you want your tea, you'll have to come back and get it."

*

Over the years since, there have been few other occasions when she has not been recognized. One was in Corsica. With the royal yacht anchored offshore, she and Philip had gone ashore for a picnic. Elizabeth, taking a short walk on her own, encountered one of the local women. The woman stopped her and, in fragmented English, asked if it was true that the Queen of England's big ship was anchored in the bay. "If you go that way, you'll be able to see it," Elizabeth told her.

Later she told Philip what had happened. "She hadn't the faintest idea who I was," she said.

"You should have told her," said Philip, grinning.

Elizabeth shook her head. "I couldn't possibly have done that."

*

Elizabeth's parents had a somewhat similar experience in the days when they were king and queen. They were at Sandringham, their country home. As always when the royals are there, the place was besieged by sightseers. For a joke, the royal couple slipped out by a side gate, walked a quarter-mile to the main gate, and mingled with those hoping to catch a glimpse of them. "Not a soul recognized us," Elizabeth's father chortled when they got back.

*

Charles, in naval uniform, was similarly unrecognized the day he was involved in a five-car pileup on his way to gunnery practice. "Buckingham Palace," he replied to one of the other drivers who asked him for his address.

*

Philip has had a number of accidental close encounters in his time. In courtship days, driving back to his naval base after an evening spent with Elizabeth, he shot off down the road in his MG and ended upside down in a ditch. Speeding through London a few days before the wedding, he was stopped by the police. "Sorry, officer" he apologized, "but I have an urgent appointment with the Archbishop of Canterbury." He was driving Elizabeth to Windsor Castle one weekend when he rammed the back of the car ahead of him. "All my fault," he conceded immediately. Another time, leaving a luncheon at which he had been the guest speaker, he banged into another car that emerged unexpectedly from a side road. And that was a particularly unfortunate encounter for a royal prince who had just made a speech on road safety.

*

Philip, on another occasion, was more than helpful to another driver whose car failed him while touring Scotland. The breakdown occurred on an incline not far from Balmoral Castle, on a stretch of road busy at the time with sightseeing cars. But no one bothered to stop and help the unfortunate man as he struggled to unhitch the trailer he was towing, until Philip chanced on the scene. "What's the trouble? Can I help?" he asked. And help he did, backing up his Land Rover so that it could be hitched to the trailer. Elizabeth, in another car, had also stopped just ahead. With the Land Rover now secured to the trailer, Philip signaled to her to carry on. Elizabeth did so, and Philip followed in the Land Rover, towing the trailer. He had just taken the strain when Elizabeth, ahead of him, was obliged to slow down. Never a man to mince words, Philip leaned out of his Land Rover. "Don't bloody stop now," he shouted.

*

Philip was equally forthright, if more jocular, the day a presentation was made to him by the Royal College of Surgeons. The presentation took the form of a silver replica of an old-fashioned bleeding bowl once used by surgeons. "That's bloody kind of you," Philip quipped in thanks.

*

He was bluntly and jocularly forthright too in Brazil when presented with the emblem of a local bowling club.

234

The club president, making the presentation, spoke in Portuguese. Philip's face showed that he did not understand a word of what was being said. In desperation, the president fell back on his few words of English. "Balls, you know," he said, handing Philip the souvenir emblem. "And balls to you, sir," Philip replied with a grin.

*

A man who once commanded his own ship, Philip was considerably frustrated in the early days of Elizabeth's reign at being compelled to play second fiddle. It showed on one occasion during their first visit to Australia. One couple presented to them at a royal function were announced as Doctor and Mr. So-and-so. Philip thought it a mistake and said so. "No mistake," said the man. "My wife has the doctorate and so is the more important."

"We have the same sort of problem in our family," sniffed Philip.

*

Philip hates feeling anything less than 100 percent fit. On the rare occasion that he has a cold he usually insists on carrying on as normal. So a Sunday that found him staying in bed at Windsor was unusual. He was clearly not well, and Elizabeth, worried, decided to send for a doctor. The doctor came, examined Philip, and found that he had a high temperature. "Stay in bed a few days," he advised. "I'll call again tomorrow."

"You'll call again when I send for you," rumbled Philip. And next day, still with a fever, he insisted on climbing out of bed and driving himself back to Buckingham Palace for business as usual.

*

Philip is not a man who suffers fools gladly. Visiting a scientific establishment on one occasion, he became

235

increasingly exasperated by the lengthy and learned jargon being trotted out. "That's all very well," he broke in eventually, "but now tell me what makes my bathwater gurgle when it goes down the plughole."

He can be affable and hail-fellow-well-met. But he can also be tetchy and moody. He was perhaps in such a frame of mind on the day he visited the docks at Liverpool. Asked if he could spare a few minutes to meet the mayors of two neighboring towns, he snapped back, "I came to meet the dockers, not your bloody mayors." To his discomfiture, his host on that occasion, Lord Derby, replied, "One of our bloody mayors is an ex-docker. The other is a railroad worker."

*

It was fortunate perhaps that it was to Elizabeth and not Philip that Walter Annenberg had to present his credentials when he arrived in London as U.S. ambassador during the Nixon administration. The formalities over, Elizabeth asked how he was settling into his new home and was amused to be told by him, "Very well, Ma'am, except for some discomfiture owing to the elements of refurbishment." Philip would have had an answer to that.

*

A man of Philip's biting wit must sometimes expect to be bitten back, and once or twice he has been. One occasion was in Calgary, Alberta. Rod Sykes, the mayor, welcomed him with the traditional gift of a white Stetson. "What, another?" sighed Philip. "Oh well, I suppose I can always use it as a flower pot." A few days later found Sykes making another presentation to Calgary's princely visitor. "I'll make a deal with you," he told Philip. "You don't ask me what to do with it and I won't tell you where to put it." With which he handed Philip a spread of steer horns measuring eighty-four inches from tip to tip.

Even blunter was the much-bemedaled Brazilian general Philip met at a state banquet in South America. "What did you get all those medals for?" Philip asked.

"I was awarded them during the war," said the general.

"I didn't know Brazil was in the war that long," sniffed Philip.

"At least, Sir, I didn't get them for marrying my wife," retorted the general.

*

If Philip can be sharp and biting at times, he can also be very human and understanding. He was occupying the royal box in the stadium at Vancouver, in Canada, the day England's Jim Peters was leading by a mile as the marathon neared its end. Peters had run himself into the ground. As he struggled toward the finish line, he collapsed several times. Each time he somehow struggled to his feet and staggered a few more yards before collapsing again. He would still have won had he not been exhausted mentally as well as physically. Yet again he collapsed...and again forced himself to his feet. But in his dazed condition, he turned and crossed the wrong finish line (used for other events). He was thus promptly disqualified and out of the medals. Philip felt that his gallant effort deserved better treatment. He himself had been given a souvenir medal of those 1954 Empire Games. As a gesture of how he felt, he had it specially mounted, inscribed "For a Very Gallant Marathon Runner," and gave it to Peters.

*

He was understanding, too, the evening he and Elizabeth took a group of friends to the theater. It was a private outing, and they wanted no fuss, the theater manager was told. Unusually for them, the royal party arrived early and took their seats in the stalls among the other playgoers. Then, just as the curtain was about to rise, two latecomers

237

arrived on the scene. Failing to recognize Elizabeth and Philip as the lights dimmed, the man said, "I think you're in the wrong seats. We have G1 and G2." Philip pulled out his own ticket stubs. "Quite right. Ours are G3 to 8," he said. He turned to Elizabeth and their friends. "Move along, everyone."

*

More than Charles, Princess Anne is a chip off the paternal block. Like Philip, she can be extremely sharp at times. "I suppose you are referring to Her Majesty the Queen," she once replied haughtily to someone who asked after her "mother." And a young man, nervous at the prospect of meeting her, fared no better when he essayed a joking remark. "I'm sorry, but I didn't quite catch the name. Anne who?" "I don't think that's at all funny," said Anne sharply.

*

Charles' years at school and in the navy have given him a better understanding than Elizabeth has of what ordinary life is really like. Even so, upbringing sometimes will out, us a local housewife discovered on one of his visits to Wales. She was in the forefront of the crowd with her two small children when, to her delight, he paused to speak to her. Delight turned to amazement, however, when Charles, conditioned by his own upbringing, inquired, "Are you the children's nanny?"

*

Diana, a week or two before she married Charles, was invited to join the royal family for the horse racing at Ascot. Only a privileged few of the racegoers there are permitted to enter the privacy of the royal enclosure, and those so privileged are issued with identifying badges by the Lord Chamberlain. "May I see your badge, please?" the gate-

238

man asked Diana as she made to enter, a request that caused her to look both startled and embarrassed. "That's Lady Diana," someone in the crowd called out. The gateman, recognizing her, blushed beet red. "I wasn't looking at faces. I was looking for badges," he mumbled.

*

It was a new, slim Diana who reappeared on the public scene following the birth of William. "You've got thin," her hatmaker, John Boyd, greeted her when she called at his premises one day.

"The word is *slim*," Diana corrected him reprovingly. "And anyhow my husband likes me this way."

*

Diana was about six months' pregnant with William the day she and Charles were scheduled to open a new cultural center together. Because Charles had a number of other engagements to fulfill before opening the cultural center, they traveled separately. Diana duly arrived at the cultural center to be greeted by the usual lineup of civic dignitaries. Hand shaking and chatting away, she made her way along the line. "I think we've met before," said a familiar voice as she extended her arm for yet another handshake. It was Charles. He had arrived unseen by Diana and had tagged on at the end of the line.

*

But the joke was on Charles the day he and Diana visited the Jaguar car plant. It was shortly after the announcement of her second pregnancy.

"Your production line here seems to be going well," Charles complimented a bunch of car workers.

"Your own production line is going well too, mate," one of them quipped back.

*

Elizabeth's mother is noted more for her human warmth than her verbal wit. But she was witty enough at one banquet she attended. An antique vase serving as the centerpiece of the table carried a Latin inscription. She asked what it meant. "I'm not sure," said her host, "but I think it says something like 'Long Live the Queen.'" Quipped Elizabeth's mother, "Perhaps we'd better get it properly translated. It may say 'To Hell with the Queen.'"

She was slyly witty, too, in South Africa in the days when her husband was still king of that country. "I find it hard to forgive the English," a disgruntled old Boer grumbled to her in the course of one of the couple's royal walkabouts.

"I understand your feeling perfectly," Elizabeth's mother replied. "I'm a Scot, you see—and the Scots find it hard to forgive the English, too."

*

More than the rest of the royal family (with the possible exception of Diana), Elizabeth's mother has what is known as the "common touch," as she clearly demonstrated the day she visited one of the poorer parts of London. One woman asked her if she would like a cup of tea. "I'd love one," she said. She went into the woman's tenement home and waited while the tea was brewed. The woman gave her a cup of tea and poured one for herself. Freshly made as it was, the tea was also very hot. Rather than wait for it to cool, the woman poured her own tea from cup to saucer, blew on it to cool it, and drank it from the saucer. Without batting an eyelid, Elizabeth's mother did the same.

*

Every summer Elizabeth's mother likes to spend a few days on her own at Sandringham, the royal family's country home. Her stay is timed to coincide with the local fur and feather show, which she always visits. She was going around the show one year when a voice in her ear asked, "Can your mother skin a rabbit?" She turned in surprise to find that she had been addressed by one of the exhibits—a myna bird. "I don't know the answer to that one," she said, smiling. To which the bird retorted, "Well, clear off then."

The following year, when she again visited the show, there was no myna bird. The show organizers had banned it on account of a new catch phrase it had picked up: "Go away, you old crow."

Wit and Wisdom

Philip is not a man who minces his words. In public, as in private, he calls a spade a spade. He once began a speech to London's Royal Zoological Society with the remark: "I apologize for any faint whiff that might emanate from this end of the room, but an orangutan has just widdled all over me."

Another speech touched on the subject of lavatories. "This is the biggest waste of water in this country by far," said Philip. "You spend half a pint and flush two gallons."

Modern art is anathema to him. "It looks like a coffin for a beatnik," he said of one exhibit in a display of British art held in San Francisco, while another reminded him of "something to hang a towel on." Even a Henry Moore bronze did not escape princely criticism. "What is it?" Philip asked, "A monkey's gallstone?"

Like a latter-day Don Quixote, he goes around tilting his verbal lance at the windmills of pomposity and complacency. He once castigated Britain's road-building program as "an absolute paradise for buck passers." British industry, he said in a radio broadcast, was like "a team with eleven coaches sitting on the bench and one player trying to cope with the oppostion." The trouble with senior management, he has opined, is that there are "too many one-ulcer men holding down two-ulcer jobs."

Architects who invited Philip to speak at their luncheon were told, "Anything which encourages you to break away from the cigar box and gasometer line ought to be encouraged." Opening a design center, he told British manufacturers, "It is no good shutting your eyes and saying 'British is best' three times a day and expecting it to be so." On another occasion he told assembled British industrialists: "We are suffering a national defeat comparable to any lost military campaign, and what is more, it is self-inflicted. Gentlemen, I think it is time we pulled our fingers out." To a gathering of military men he said: "Throughout history the basic qualification for officers has been the ability to handle men. Modern warfare has added two other requirements—the ability to handle machines and the ability to handle paper."

Even the American language has not escaped his biting wit. "We can take pride in the fact that he speaks English," he said at a dinner in honor of America's General Gruenther, former Supreme Allied Commander in Europe, "or perhaps I had better put it that he speaks a language we can all understand."

Understandably, Philip's speeches sometimes upset his listeners. Canadians were not best pleased when he said in Canada: "It is a complete misconception to imagine that the monarchy exists in the interests of the monarchy. It does not. It exists in the interests of people in the sense that we do not come here for our health. We can think of better ways of enjoying ourselves."

Not a few women in Britain were similarly offended when Philip said: "British women can't cook. They are very good at decorating food and making it attractive, but they have an inability to cook."

And Britain's Labor government of earlier years did not like it when Philip said: "People say this is a permissive society, but we live in the most regimented society ever in this country. You practically have to have a license to breathe."

*

Philip writes his own speeches. His threefold maxim for a good speech is "Brevity—Simplicity—Humor." It is better that a speech should bore people rather than upset them, he says, though he himself does not always practice what he preaches in this respect. What he has to say does sometimes upset his listeners, and he knows it, as he admitted to a gathering of students: "I get kicked in the teeth often enough for saying things I am told I damned well ought not to say."

This happens so frequently that he jokes of having invented a new science—dontopedics. "It means putting your foot in your mouth," explains Philip.

*

There has been more than a grain of truth—and sometimes a touch of wisdom—in some of Philip's speeches. These are among the things he has said.

On bringing up children: "It is very easy when children want something to say no immediately. I think it is import-ant not to give an unequivocal answer at once. Much better to think it over. Then if you say no, they really accept it."

On education: "The art of education is to combine formal training with as wide a variety of experiences as possible, including some which involve a calculated risk."

On democracy: "I have noticed a growing tendency in many parts of the Free World for ordinary people to be pushed around by authority, supposedly for their own good."

On the permissive society: "It is becoming only too apparent that it is possible for communities to achieve quite high standards of material development with at the same time the moral and behavorial standards of a colony of monkeys."

On international sport: "So many countries see success as a means of gaining international prestige or as an advertisement for political theory or ideology that competition is simply a means to an end. They are not always so scrupulous about the means either."

On freedom: "I see no advantage in a prosperous and powerful state if it is to be achieved at the expense of human freedom and happiness. Controls, restrictions, and limitations do nothing but inhibit change and discourage enterprise. Experience and history have shown that restriction on one section of the community has a way of growing into restrictions on all sections of the community."

On Britain (at a luncheon in New York): "Britain is not just an old country of tottering ruins inhabited by idle roués in eyeglasses. Nor is it a country where yokels quaff ale by the tankard outside rickety pubs, where all the soldiers are dressed in scarlet tunics and spend all their time marching up and down for the benefit of visitors."

On monarchy: "One of its greatest weaknesses...is that it has to be all things to all people. It cannot do this when it comes to being all things to people who are traditionalists and all things to people who are iconoclasts. We therefore find ourselves in a position of compromise, and we might be kicked by both sides."

On innovation: "There are always twenty excellent reasons for doing nothing for every one reason for starting anything—especially if it has never been done before."

On argument: "Whereas an intelligent man with an open mind can demolish a bad idea by reasoned argument, those who allow their brains to atrophy resort to meaningless catch phrases, derision, and finally anger in the face of anything new."

Philip on Philip: "I am one of those stupid bums who

never went to university." "I am one of the generation who started the war in nappies [diapers], spent the next eight years in uniform, and when peace broke out found myself without any clothing." "I am one of the most governed people in the world." "I haven't got a job; I am self-employed." "I am quite used to an eighteen-hour day." "The work [as consort] has turned out ten times tougher than I expected, but I am ten times happier than I expected to be."

*

If Philip's wit is sometimes exercised at the expense of others, he has also been known to tell the occasional joke against himself. One such joke recalled the time his wartime destroyer was berthed alongside a Canadian destroyer. The crews of the two ships were on such good terms, said Philip, that "we soon lost track of where one hangover ended and the next began."

He also indulged rather too freely, he has joked, on an official visit to Edinburgh. "We were just about to leave when someone said that the train was twenty minutes late. The Lord Provost rushed round and refilled the glasses. As we were finishing, someone said the train was still twenty minutes late. This continued for some time, and eventually the train was six drinks late. When we came out of the hotel many citizens must have marveled to see the Lord Provost and myself on such extremely good terms."

*

Like Philip, Charles insists on writing his own speeches and has done so from the age of twenty, when he made his first major speech, an address at the Gandhi centenary celebrations. Young and inexperienced as Charles was at the time, his great-uncle, Earl Mountbatten, thought he would welcome having his speech drafted for him. To his astonishment, Charles, after scanning the speech Uncle

Dickie had prepared, handed it back to him. "I wonder if you would mind terribly if I didn't use this," he said. "I'd rather write my own."

*

Like Philip, too, Charles leavens his speechs with a touch of humor. But where Philip can be bitingly witty, Charles is sometimes uproariously funny. "I am often asked whether it is because of some genetic trait that I stand with my hands behind my back, like my father," he said in a speech to the Master Tailors' Benevolent Association. "The answer is that we both have the same tailor. He makes our sleeves so tight that we can't get our hands in front."

To appreciate another of his jokes, you have to know something of the tongue-twisting pronunciation of the Welsh language. Place names are especially difficult. The town of Llanelli, for instance, is pronounced Cla-neth-li. which gave Charles the basis for his joke. "When I went to Llanelli not long ago, the mayor said, 'Can you say "Llanelli"?' So I said, 'Llanelli.' He wiped the saliva out of his eye and said, 'Well done.'"

That was on television. For a radio program on Wales, Charles turned reporter himself. Among the people he interviewed was a Welsh farmer. Conversation turned to the subject of artificial insemination in animals. Quipped Charles, "It's so unfair on the rams and bulls. They get terrible psychological problems, I'm told."

Visiting the Royal Thames Yacht Club to unveil a bust of Prince Philip, he concluded a brief speech with the quip: "I now complete the process of helping my father to expose himself." And in a speech to a university debating society he joked, "I hear that in America they spray so much insecticide around that even cannibals have begun to complain that Americans taste of DDT."

*

But the joke was on Charles in a speech he made while he and Diana were in Australia in 1983. Researching a speech he was to make to an audience of 3,000 schoolchildren at an open-air rally, he came across some words of advice a nineteenth-century Australian mother had given to her children, and he decided to embody her words of advice in his speech. He was busy quoting from her, warning his young listeners against aggression and falsehood, telling them not to be bad-tempered or spiteful, when a gust of wind carried his notes away. "God, my bloody bit of paper," he exclaimed—and the amplifying system relayed the remark clearly to his youthful audience. His notes were retrieved and handed back to him. To his considerable embarrassment, he then found that the next piece of advice he had to pass on to the children consisted of the words: "Swearing is contemptible and foolish."

*

Just as Philip resents the media image of himself as "an uncultured clot"—his own words—so Charles dislikes being thought of as no more than a princely clown or playboy. There are no jokes when he speaks on subjects close to his heart. This is what he had to say on the subject of freedom:

"The most insidious enemies of liberty are those who tell us that they know us and our true needs better than we do ourselves. For they are wise and we are foolish or blind or misled. One day we shall grow up—as a result of obeying their orders—and we shall then realise how right they were to coerce us in our own interest. If we mind about what we call freedom, what exactly are we trying to preserve? Surely it is our right not to be treated as a collective mass which can be manipulated as so much malleable human material. Presumably we wish to avoid becoming like bricks to be constructed by the infallible architect—bricks which, if they do not fit, must be eliminated or reeducated."

Charles believes strongly, too, in the value of alternative medicine. "When it comes to healing people," he said in one speech, "it seems to me that account has to be taken of those sometimes long-neglected methods of medicine which, in the right hands, can bring considerable relief if not hope to an increasing number of people."

And he has firm ideas, stemming from his own disciplined upbringing, on how to bring out the best in the young. "If young people are placed in a disciplined environment, presented with challenging circumstances and pushed beyond themselves, the results can be quite extraordinary. Suddenly they find hidden corners in their characters which they never knew existed. They develop talents and gifts which would otherwise never have materialized. They develop self-confidence and self-reliance."

*

He also feels strongly about George III, the last British king who was also king of America, an ancestor who, Charles believes, has been misrepresented by history. "The view that is prevalent in schools," Charles has said, "is that George III was the mad king who lost the American colonies. That is all people seem to know about him. I feel it is very unfortunate if one is misunderstood in history. I should hate that what happened in an international sense should mask him as a person, a human being, someone who was a great patron of the arts, a great family man, someone who was enormously loved and respected. I would not say that George III was mad. I think it has been fairly conclusively proved that he was suffering from a metabolic condition [porphyria] which affected his blood and to a certain extent his mind."

*

Charles on himself: "The most important thing a person in my position can have is a sense of humor, being able to laugh at oneself." "I am not a rebel by temperament." "There is no set of rules as to what my job is. I am heir to the throne—full stop. I could do absolutely nothing if I wanted to. I could go and play polo all over the world. All the things I have got myself involved in I do because I am interested or concerned or anxious." "In company with convicts, lunatics, and peers of the realm, I am ineligible to vote." "I always feel that it is worth challenging yourself, and this is what I do most of the time, perhaps to too great an extent."

*

Diana has so far remained shy of speech making, displaying her wit only in the occasional off-the-cuff remark, sometimes at her husband's expense. Telling people about William during the course of one walkabout, she said, "He takes after his father—he dribbles." In Canada, shown a flag dating from Queen Victoria's day, she quipped, "It's as old as my husband." In Britain, presented with a giant teddy bear, she inquired slyly, "Is it for my husband or our baby?" Others besides Charles are sometimes on the receiving end of her humor. "Which of you put it on your expense account?" she teased newsmen and photographers when they presented her with a bouquet at the end of a photo session. And she had a quip at her own expense while being measured for a hat. Her head is on the large side. "It may be large, but there's not much in it," she joked.

*

Elizabeth has made numerous speeches over her years of monarchy, mostly written for her by others. Jokes in her public speeches are noted mainly for their absence. Her speeches are designed to avoid controversy and, in consequence, seldom include anything that is likely to go down in history. But she was clearly speaking from the heart when she gave her views on marriage in the speech she made on her silver wedding anniversary:

"A marriage begins by joining man and wife together. But this relationship, however deep, needs to develop and mature with the passing years. For this it must be held firm in the web of family relationships—between parents and children, grandparents and grandchildren, cousins, aunts and uncles."

She spoke from the heart, too, when unveiling a memorial to her dead father, King George VI. "Much was asked of my father in personal sacrifice and endeavor, often in the face of illness," she said. "His courage in overcoming it endeared him to everybody. He shirked no task, however difficult, and to the end he never faltered in his duty to his peoples. Through all the strains of his public life he remained a man of warm and friendly sympathies, a man who by the simple qualities of loyalty, resolution, and service won for himself such a place in the affection of all of us that when he died millions mourned for him as for a true and trusted friend."

*

Because the queen is not good at small talk, jokes do not spring readily to her lips even on walkabouts. But there has been the occasional quip. "Thank you, Sir Walter Raleigh," she said to the deputy mayor of Auckland, New Zealand, when she was caught in a summer shower and he offered her his raincoat. "The ideal place for an assignation," she murmered as she was shown around the dimly lighted nocturnal mammal house at the London Zoo.

But the best of her jokes are uttered in private. "I wouldn't be surprised if their children are four-legged," she quipped when her horse-mad daughter, Anne, married the equally horse-mad Mark Phillips.

Anne's occasional speeches are mostly brief and platitudinous. Casual remarks are more revealing. She regards pregnancy, she says, as "an occupational hazard for a wife" and talks of horse riding as "the one thing I do well and can be seen to do well." At various times she has confessed:

"I am not particularly maternal."

"I am academically lazy."

"My back view isn't very good."

Anne once told a young man who partnered her at a dance, "I'm not made of Dresden china. I won't break." She takes the view that "there are always people around waiting for me to put my foot in it, just like my father."

She is noted for being more temperamental than humorous, but the occasional joke is not totally unknown. "I'd love one of these for Christmas," she quipped after driving a fifty-three-ton army tank across country. Presented with a ceremonial key while visiting Gambia in 1984, she joked, "I promise not to rampage through the city with it."

*

Of all the royal family, Elizabeth's mother, born at the turn of the century, is the most philosophical. "Your mother is more than merely clever," Elizabeth was once told by her father. "She is wise." Charles shares this view of his grandmother. She has "a golden touch," he says.

When the Duke of Windsor abdicated and Elizabeth's parents unexpectedly found themselves king and queen, her father was so disturbed at the prospect that he broke down and wept. "We must take what is coming to us and make the best of it," Elizabeth's mother comforted him. Those who worked for the couple were equally alarmed at what the changeover would involve. "Only circumstances change," Elizabeth's mother reassured them. "People remain the same."

*

The queen mother has a maxim of her own devising for almost every situation and circumstance. Here are some of them:

"A quiet man should not be mistaken for a weak one."

"Your work is the rent you pay for the room you occupy on earth."

"Being royal is no excuse for bad manners."

"Half the fun of being a grandmother is being able to spoil your grandchildren."

But spoiling your grandchildren, in her view, does not mean that they should have everything their own way, as Charles discovered when, unhappy in schooldays, he begged her to intercede with his parents and persuade them to let him leave Gordonstoun. Instead, she told him, "We all have to do things in life we don't like. We simply have to buckle down and make the best of it."

Royal Firsts

The first British monarch to hand out titles to those who served him loyally was William the Conqueror when he made himself King of England as well as Duke of Normandy in 1066.

*

First king to employ numeration in order to distinguish himself from a previous king with the same name was the Edward who succeeded to the crown in 1284. He called himself Edward II to avoid confusion with his father, Edward Longshanks.

*

First king to have a prime minister was George I. Before that kings had been their own prime ministers. But George, fresh from Hanover, was hampered in his political dealings by the fact that he could speak hardly a word of English. So he had to have a prime minister to do his speaking for him.

*

The first of Elizabeth's ancestors to live in Buckingham Palace was George III. A much smaller red-brick residence in those days, it was called simply Buckingham House when he bought it for $25,000.

*

Queen Victoria was the first royal to have anesthetic in childbirth. She had chloroform when the eighth of her nine children, Prince Leopold, was born in 1853, and her example gave a big boost to the pioneering work for easier childbirth.

*

Queen Victoria was also the first of the family to make a public appearance on the palace's now-famous balcony. She stood on the balcony to take the salute when British troops marched off to fight in the Crimean War. The tradition of royal balcony appearances at times of national crisis or rejoicing has continued since.

*

First royal couple to kiss on the balcony in public were Charles and Diana, after their 1981 wedding. It was Andrew who egged them into it. "Go on—give her a kiss," he whispered to Charles.

*

First of the family to be cited in a divorce action was the womanizing King Edward VII. As a young Prince of Wales, he was involved when Sir Charles Mordaunt brought divorce proceedings against his twenty-one-year-old wife, Harriet, after she had confessed to having "done very wrong" with a number of men—Lord Cole, Sir Frederick Johnstone, and a Captain Farquhar, as well as the Prince of Wales. Servants of the couple gave evidence that the prince frequently called to see Harriet when her husband was away, but Bertie himself swore on oath in court that there had been no "improper familiarity."

*

Edward VII was also the first king to own a car, a two-cylinder six-horse-power Daimler with an open body that he bought in 1900. The first time he went out in it, a groom on horseback rode ahead. But the car soon overtook the horse, and the king promptly ordered the groom to return to the stables. Such a display of impetuousity naturally worried royal aides, and they gave secret orders to the king's chauffeur that he must always drive as slowly as possible. This did not suit Bertie at all. "Faster, man, faster," he would roar at the unfortunate chauffeur. That first-ever royal car is today preserved in the museum at Sandringham, the family's country home.

*

First royal to make a radio breakfast broadcast was Elizabeth's grandfather, King George V. He first broadcast at Christmas 1932, and continued to make an annual Christmas broadcast until 1935, a few weeks before he died. Worried on account of his stammer, Elizabeth's father, when he succeeded to the throne, at first discontinued this new royal tradition, but reestablished it from the first Christmas of World War II. Elizabeth II, when she ascended to the throne, continued it in turn.

*

First of the family to learn to fly were Elizabeth's father and his eldest brother, then Prince of Wales and later Duke of Windsor. Both went solo for the first time in 1929, though Windsor had had his own airplane for some years before that, a Bristol fighter with dual controls and an airforce pilot.

*

First of the actual royal family to die in an air crash was Elizabeth's uncle, George, Duke of Kent. He was on his way to visit British troops in Iceland during World War II when his Sunderland flying boat ploughed into a Scottish hillside in heavy cloud and exploded. Of the fifteen men

257

aboard, only the tailgunner survived. However, Philip had previously known what it was to lose a close relative in an air crash. He was still a schoolboy at Gordonstoun in the 1930s when his sister Cecilie, her husband, the Grand Duke of Hesse, and their two children all perished in an air crash. They were flying to London to attend a wedding when they ran into fog over Ostend and their aircraft hit a factory chimney.

*

Elizabeth's coronation in 1953 was the first to be televised. Her advisers were against the idea, but she insisted. She wanted the nation to share the occasion with her, she said. In fact, there were only a few thousand television sets in Britain at the time.

*

First of the royal family to appear personally on television was Prince Philip. That was in 1957 when he gave a talk entitled "Round the World in Forty Minutes" based on his Antarctic expedition. As the title suggests, the program was scheduled to last 40 minutes. In fact, despite trembling with nerves, Philip stretched it out to 55 minutes. "Overtime, as usual," he quipped. His example encouraged Elizabeth to make her first telecast when she was in Canada later that year.

*

Charles was the first heir to the throne ever to go to school. It was his father's idea. Before that, royal offspring had always been educated by private governesses and tutors.

*

First royal not to promise to obey her husband in her wedding-day vows was the Danish-born wife of Elizabeth's cousin Richard, Duke of Gloucester. Strictly speaking, of course, she did not actually become one of the royal family until the completion of the wedding ceremony. Following her example, Diana also elected not to say "obey" when she married Charles.

*

First royal prince to be born in a hospital was Diana's firstborn, William. Princess Anne and the Danish-born Duchess of Gloucester had previously gone into the hospital for childbirth, but their babies were not princes or princesses.

*

William was also the first royal baby ever to go on tour. He was only nine months when Charles and Diana took him with them to Australia and New Zealand in 1983.

*

And a notable last. Last British king to lead his troops into battle was George II. Sword in hand, shouting, "Now, boys, for the honor of England," he led a cavalry charge against the French at Dettingen in 1743.

Historical Footnotes

Elizabeth II is the sixty-second sovereign of England and the seventh queen to occupy the throne in her own right since Egbert the Great first united the country's warring tribes (or most of them) back in Saxon times. She has been queen since February 6, 1952, but still has a long way to go to rival the reign of her great-great-grandmother, Queen Victoria.

*

Queen Victoria ranks as the longest-reigning monarch in British history. She reigned for 63 years, 216 days. She was also the longest-lived monarch, being 81 years, 243 days old when she died in 1901. By contrast, the youthful King Edward V was a boy of twelve when he vanished into the Tower of London in 1483 to be seen no more.

*

The shortest reign was that of Queen Jane (Lady Jane Grey). She had been on the throne only nine days at the tender age of sixteen when she was overthrown, and later executed, by Mary Tudor. The Duke of Windsor reigned as King Edward VIII for 325 days in 1936 before abdicating to marry Wallis Simpson.

*

Anne of Cleves, fourth wife of King Henry VIII, served the shortest term of any queen consort. Henry married and divorced "the Flemish mare," as he called her, all in the space of 184 days. In all, Henry VIII had six wives. He beheaded two for alleged infidelity, divorced two, saw one die in childbirth, and was outlived by the sixth.

*

Queen Anne had the most children—seventeen in all, though only one survived infancy. Edward I sired sixteen legitimate offspring plus several bastards. Henry I had even more bastards—certainly twenty and possibly twenty-two—by a succession of six mistresses, but only two legitimate children by his wife, Queen Matilda. Charles II had more mistresses, at least nine and possibly more, by whom he sired some fourteen or fifteen illegitimate children (history is uncertain on the point).

*

The oldest monarch ever to ascend to the throne was William IV. He was nearly sixty-five when he became king in 1830. Charles could be as old, or even older, if Elizabeth II outlives Victoria. The youngest-ever monarch was King Henry VI. He was a mere nine months when he became king and grew up into a pious weakling who crept around at night spying on his servants to ensure that they were not making love.

*

It is only in comparatively recent times that the royals have become the highly moral family they are today. Elizabeth's uncle, the Duke of Windsor, shared his favors between two long-term mistresses before Wallis Simpson came into his life. Elizabeth's great-grandfather, Edward VII, proudly paraded a succession of mistresses in public, among them the actress Lillie Langtry. He even had a group of them sitting together at his coronation. "The king's loosebox," his friends styled the batch of seats allocated to his royal mistresses.

*

George I, when he traveled to Britain from Germany to take over the throne, left his wife behind in Hanover, imprisoned because she had had an affair with a Swedish count. Instead, he took two mistresses to London with him, one so stout and the other so thin that his English subjects promptly nicknamed them "the Elephant" and "the Maypole."

*

George IV had a penchant for actresses. A particular favorite was Mary Robinson, who used the stage name of Perdita. His brother, William IV, also had an actress as a mistress, Dorothea Jordan, by whom he had not fewer than ten children. George IV was later infatuated by Maria Fitzherbert, a twice-widowed Catholic, whom he actually married when he was Prince of Wales. The marriage was illegal under the Royal Marriages Act, and shortage of money later forced him to toe the royal line and marry his cousin, Princess Caroline of Brunswick. They spent only one night together before separating, George returning to Maria while Caroline took off to lead a life of promiscuity in Italy.

*

Charles II collected mistresses as other men collect hunting trophies, starting at the age of fifteen with the Governor of Bridgwater's wife. Over the years ahead his collection was to include duchesses and actresses, a chaplain's daughter, and one of his wife's bridesmaids. Perhaps the most famous of his mistresses were the actresses Moll Davis and Nell Gwynn. They were rivals both on stage and in the royal bedchamber. One night when it was Moll's turn to sleep with the king, Nell ensured that there would be no lovemaking by giving her rival a batch of sweetmeats laced with a purgative. At one stage, Nell also found herself competing for the king's favors with Louise de Keroualle, a French-born Catholic. She was driving through London one day when her carriage became the target of a bombardment of rotten fruit. "Stop it, you fools," shouted Nell, poking her head out of the carriage window. "I'm the Protestant whore, not the Catholic one."

*

Many of Elizabeth's ancestors came to violent or untimely ends:

- Two of the early Saxon kings—Edmund and Edward the Martyr—were assassinated.
- Harold was hacked to pieces at the Battle of Hastings.
- William the Conqueror's son, William Rufus, was shot dead with an arrow.
- Richard the Lionhearted died from gangrene after being wounded by a crossbow bolt.
- The homosexual Edward II was disemboweled with a red-hot poker on the orders of his wife and her lover.
- Edward III died of gonorrhea.
- Henry IV died of leprosy.
- Richard II was murdered.
- Henry VI was either murdered or executed, according to which side you were on at the time.
- The young Edward V and his still younger brother vanished into the Tower of London and were never seen again. It was another 150 years before their remains were discovered, buried ten feet down.

- Richard III, who is popularly supposed to have been responsible for their deaths, was himself slain with a battle-axe at the Battle of Bosworth.
- Henry VIII died of syphilis.
- Sixteen-year-old Jane Grey was beheaded along with her husband.
- Charles I was also beheaded. He wore two shirts when he went to his execution on a bitterly cold January morning. He did not want people to think he shivered with fear, he said.
- William III died as a result of being thrown from his horse when it stumbled on a molehill.
- George IV and his brother, William IV, both died from cirrhosis of the liver, while George II's son, Frederick, died before he could become king by being struck on the head by a cricket ball.

*

If Elizabeth II's long and historic ancestry is dotted with bad kings and sad queens, Britain has also had monarchs who have been good, strong, and wise. Egbert the Great united the warring tribes of England into a single nation. Edward I welded England, Scotland, and Wales into Britain. William the Conqueror built the Tower of London. Elizabeth I and James I encouraged the settlement of Virginia. George III founded those two world-famous institutions, the Royal Academy and the Royal Botanical Gardens. And Queen Victoria's husband, the intellectual Prince Albert, stepped in to prevent war between Britain and America.

It was during the early stages of the American Civil War when a Federal sloop-of-war, the *San Jacinto*, intercepted the English mail steamer *Trent* and arrested two Confederate envoys who were aboard bound for London and Paris. Lord Palmerston, Britain's Foreign Secretary,

265

promptly drafted an indignant protest. Albert, chancing to see the letter of protest before it was sent, was horrified. Worded as it was, he said, it made it impossible for President Lincoln to back down without losing face, and he took it upon himself to draft it afresh in more diplomatic terms. As a result of his intervention, the two Confederate envoys were released and war between the two countries— Britain was already embarking troops for Canada—was averted.